creating a web site
with flash cs4
professional

Visual QuickProject Guide

by David Morris

Peachpit Press

Visual QuickProject Guide
Creating a Web Site with Flash CS4 Professional
David Morris

Peachpit Press

1249 Eighth Street
Berkeley, CA 94710
510/524-2178
510/524-2221 (fax)

Find us on the Web at: www.peachpit.com
To report errors, please send a note to: errata@peachpit.com
Peachpit Press is a division of Pearson Education.

Editor: Rebecca Gulick
Copy Editors: Liz Welch and Anne Marie Walker
Production Coordinator: Becky Winter
Compositors: David Morris, Becky Winter, Roberta Great
Indexer: Rebecca Plunkett
Technical Reviewer: Jeremy Rue
Cover photo credit: Daniel Loiselle

ISBN 13: 978-0-321-59151-7
ISBN 10:   0-321-59151-8

9 8 7 6 5 4 3 2 1

Printed and bound in the United States of America

for the better d of the double d's

Special Thanks to...

Liz Dobecka and Timeless Blooms, for letting me use the business one last time.

Courtney and Michael, the happy couple. The beauty of your special day makes my work look that much better.

Good friends—old and new.

Liz Welch and Anne Marie Walker for making me look literate and Jeremy Rue for keeping me accurate.

Rebecca Gulick, Becky Winter, and everyone at Peachpit for their infinite patience and support.

contents

5. use the timeline to organize your site   41

6. add animation to your web site   53

7. build a navigation system   75

8. add inside sections of the web site   95

contents

introduction

The Visual QuickProject Guide that you hold in your hands offers a unique way to learn about new technologies. Instead of drowning you in theoretical possibilities and lengthy explanations, this Visual QuickProject Guide uses big, color illustrations coupled with clear, concise step-by-step instructions to show you how to complete one specific project in a matter of hours.

Our project in this book is to create a beautiful, engaging Web site using Adobe Flash CS4 Professional. Our Web site showcases a small, home-based business. But since the project covers all the basic techniques, you'll be able to use what you learn to create your own Flash-based Web sites—perhaps to promote your own business, showcase a hobby or collection, or provide a site for your neighborhood association.

what you'll create

This is the home page of the Timeless Blooms Web site, the project you'll create. In the process, you'll learn the following useful techniques:

Draw graphic elements to define your site's look and feel.

Use special text containers to process user input and load text dynamically.

Create interactive buttons for navigation between the different sections of your site.

Animate text to provide interest and a professional quality.

Format text in the font, size, and color of your choice.

Import graphics and images created in other applications.

Import video, including cue points that trigger changes in your movie.

Parse XML files to create a dynamic photo gallery.

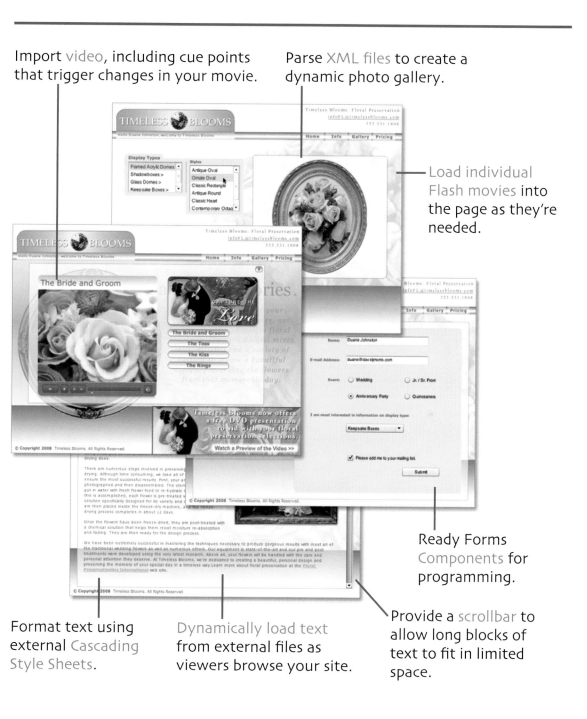

Load individual Flash movies into the page as they're needed.

Ready Forms Components for programming.

Provide a scrollbar to allow long blocks of text to fit in limited space.

Format text using external Cascading Style Sheets.

Dynamically load text from external files as viewers browse your site.

how this book works

The title of each section explains what is covered in that section.

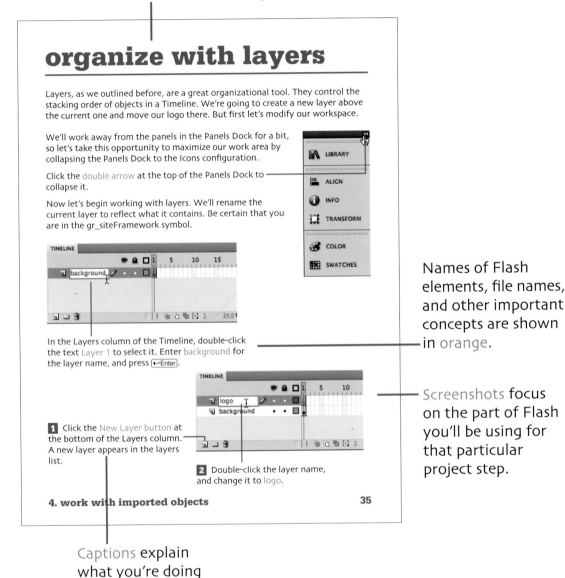

organize with layers

Layers, as we outlined before, are a great organizational tool. They control the stacking order of objects in a Timeline. We're going to create a new layer above the current one and move our logo there. But first let's modify our workspace.

We'll work away from the panels in the Panels Dock for a bit, so let's take this opportunity to maximize our work area by collapsing the Panels Dock to the Icons configuration.

Click the double arrow at the top of the Panels Dock to collapse it.

Now let's begin working with layers. We'll rename the current layer to reflect what it contains. Be certain that you are in the gr_siteFramework symbol.

In the Layers column of the Timeline, double-click the text Layer 1 to select it. Enter background for the layer name, and press [↵Enter].

Names of Flash elements, file names, and other important concepts are shown in orange.

1 Click the New Layer button at the bottom of the Layers column. A new layer appears in the layers list.

2 Double-click the layer name, and change it to logo.

Screenshots focus on the part of Flash you'll be using for that particular project step.

4. work with imported objects

35

Captions explain what you're doing and why.

The extra bits section at the end of chapters contains additional tips and tricks that you might like to know but that aren't absolutely necessary for creating the Web page.

extra bits

reusable graphics p. 26

- Using symbols in Flash provides two main benefits: reduced file size and ease of editing.

  When you create a symbol and place instances of that symbol on the Stage, your movie's file size is reduced because no matter how many times you use it, the code required to define it is only included in the file once. Each instance just points to the symbol and describes any modifications to that symbol, such as transparency or size.

  Modifying work later is also much easier. Imagine that you've placed 100 blue squares (not instances of a blue square symbol) throughout your movie, and then you decide to change the color. You have to find and change all 100 squares. But if you made a symbol of a blue square and placed 100 instances, you only have to change the symbol, and the 100 instances are updated automatically.

symbol-editing mode p. 30

- When you have an object on the Stage that is a container for other objects (groups, symbols, and text boxes), you can just double-click it to "get inside" and edit the contents.

- To exit the editing mode of the container, you can double-click outside the bounds of the container or use the Edit bar.

transform objects p. 31

- When you're scaling vector objects (those drawn in Flash or imported from Illustrator or Fireworks, as in the logo file.) you can increase or decrease the size without any negative effects. However, if you're working with a bitmap image, you'll want to avoid enlarging it. An enlarged bitmap has to be resampled and can become distorted or fuzzy. It's best to open the image in an image editor such as Adobe Photoshop and scale it to the size you need.

The heading for each group of tips matches the section title. (The colors are just for decoration and have no hidden meaning.)

Next to the heading there's a page number that also shows which section the tips belong to.

4. work with imported objects

companion web site

You can find the companion Web site for Creating a Web Site with Flash CS4 Professional: Visual QuickProject Guide at: http://www.davidjmorris.com/vqj/flash.

In the Asset Files section of the site, you'll find all the files you need to complete the project in this book. You can also download the intermediate files created in each chapter and the files that make up the final project site.

Visit the Completed Project Site section to see a completed example of the site you're building in this book.

You can also find any updated material in the Corrections section of the site.

explore flash

At first glance, the Flash interface can be overwhelming with its many panels and controls, but don't be concerned. As you progress through this project, you'll learn how to access the important stuff and how to harness all the power of Flash. When you finish the project, you'll have the knowledge and skills needed to create a professional-quality Web site to suit your business, organization, or personal needs.

Flash borrows many of its conventions and terms from film production. The presentation you create for viewers is a movie, the distinct parts of the movie are scenes, the players (your content) are on the Stage, and movement through time is accomplished via the Timeline. Thinking about the Flash interface in the context of this film metaphor will help you quickly grasp the way we work in Flash. We are producing a movie that features your content and tells the story you want Web viewers to see. (See extra bits on page xx.)

explore flash (cont.)

In Flash, you'll often find yourself drilled down multiple levels within elements, such as when editing text that is inside a button symbol inside a movie placed in a particular scene. The Edit Bar above the Stage displays those levels to help keep you oriented and to let you quickly backtrack when your edit is complete. Additionally, you can use it to navigate between scenes, to locate and modify symbols, and to change view magnification.

Gray space around the Stage makes up the Pasteboard, which holds objects that hang off the Stage and animated elements that move onto or off the Stage. To view or hide objects on the Pasteboard, choose View > Work Area, or press Ctrl Shift w (Windows) or ⌘ Shift w (Mac).

The story you're telling with your movie is presented on the Stage. You'll use it as your workspace to place and arrange the elements of your site. The Stage's rectangular dimensions define the area of your movie that viewers will see.

The Tools panel is the toolbox you'll use to draw objects, create text, and modify the elements of your movie. The Tools panel also lets you modify colors and set options for the tools you choose.

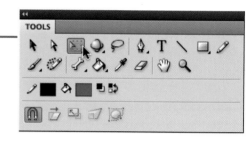

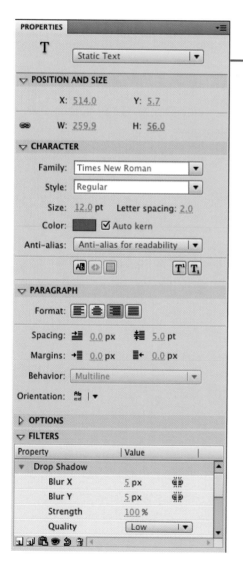

Review and change the attributes of objects in the Property Inspector. Controls in the Property Inspector are organized into sections and change dynamically, displaying the attributes and settings relevant to your current selection. Here you'll be able to modify the attributes of text, graphics, frames, animations, and more.

explore flash (cont.)

The Timeline controls the order, timing, and flow of your movie. The panel contains three primary sections: frames, layers, and the Playhead.

The layer and frame of objects selected on the stage are identified with highlights.

The Playhead indicates the current frame displayed on the Stage.

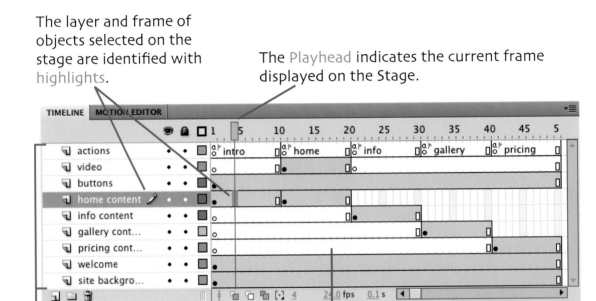

Think of layers as independent strips of film, each containing its own objects-stacked on top of one another-and composited to present a particular frame. In most cases, each layer we create will contain only a few objects, making it easier to keep track of things as the project gets progressively more complex.

Frames in the Timeline represent changes in your content over time. However, it's important to think of frames as something more than just for animation; frames also serve an important function as milestones within your site to which you can link other content.

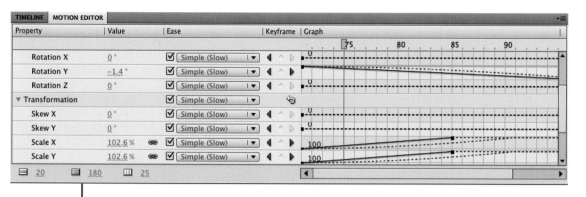

The Motion Editor provides detailed control over all tween properties and their property keyframes, including rotation, size, scale, position, filters, and more. You can create a tween in the Timeline or use Motion Presets and then refine it in the Motion Editor. After Effects users will appreciate the familiar interface paradigm.

```
ACTIONS - FRAME

                                                          Script Assist  ?
// Add a listener object to the btnClose instance.
// Execute function hideScreen on click.
videoScreen.btnClose.addEventListener(MouseEvent.CLICK, hideScreen);
function hideScreen(evt:Event):void {
    videoScreen.theVideo.stop();
    videoScreen.visible=false;
}

videoScreen.theVideo.addEventListener(MetadataEvent.CUE_POINT, cuePointListener);
function cuePointListener(event:MetadataEvent):void {
    var cueName=event.info.name;
    videoScreen.tfHeader.text=cueName;
    videoScreen.mcVideoBanner.gotoAndStop(cueName);
}

videoScreen.btnBandG.addEventListener(MouseEvent.CLICK, seekBandG);
function seekBandG(evt:Event):void {
    videoScreen.theVideo.seekToNavCuePoint("The Bride and Groom");
}

videoScreen.btnToss.addEventListener(MouseEvent.CLICK, seekToss);
function seekToss(evt:Event):void {
    videoScreen.theVideo.seekToNavCuePoint("The Toss");
}

Line 47 of 59, Col 1
```

The Actions panel is used for adding ActionScript to your movie. ActionScript is Flash's scripting language for adding complex interactivity, controlling navigation, and programming many of the advanced functions found in robust Flash applications.

introduction

explore flash (cont.)

If the elements in your movie are the players, then symbols are the featured stars. Using symbols decreases file size, saves time on edits, and organizes your file. The symbols in your movie are stored and accessed from the Library panel.

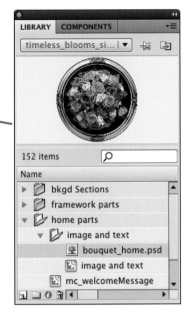

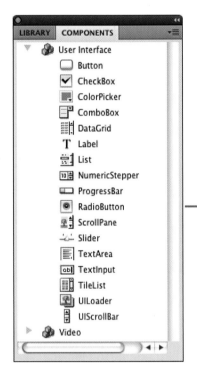

Components, accessed from the Components panel, are packages of special-purpose objects that include the ActionScript to control their behavior. Components include simple user interface controls, such as buttons and check boxes, and more complex controls that contain content, such as scroll panes, windows, and video players.

After you add a component to your file, you'll use the Component Inspector panel to specify parameters specific to the component type and your particular design requirements.

the next step

While this Visual QuickProject Guide teaches you the basics for creating a Web site in Flash, there is much more to learn. If you're curious about Flash development, try Flash CS4 Professional for Windows and Macintosh: Visual QuickStart Guide (Peachpit Press, 2009), by Katherine Ulrich. It features clear examples, simple step-by-step instructions, and loads of visual aids to cover every aspect of Flash design.

After that, you can take it to the next level with Flash CS4 Professional Advanced for Windows and Macintosh: Visual QuickPro Guide (Peachpit Press, 2009), by Russell Chun.

extra bits

explore flash p.xiii

- Avoid the temptation to "store" unused objects offstage on the Pasteboard; they'll still be exported in the final movie and will add to the file size, prolonging download times.

- Need a custom user interface element that's not included in Flash installed components? Many custom components can be found on the Adobe Exchange for you to download and install. The Exchange is located at: http://www.adobe.com/exchange.

1. prepare your site files

Before you begin the design and development of your Web site, it's important to get organized.

In this chapter, we set up a directory structure for all of our files, create and save the Flash file that will be our site movie, and define and save the color scheme that we'll use throughout the site.

If you haven't already done so, download the asset files for the Timeless Blooms Web site from this book's companion site at www.davidjmorris.com/vqj/flash.

define folder structure

Before beginning work on our Flash movie, you need to set up a hierarchy of folders and files on your computer's desktop. Within this structure we'll have two discrete folder sets: one for files that we'll use during the development of the site and one for files that will be uploaded to the Web.

From the Windows Explorer or Mac OS's Finder, choose File > New > Folder to create the parent directory. Name the folder timeless_blooms_website.

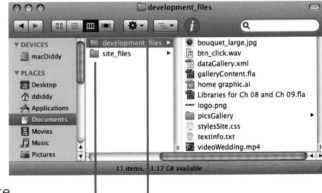

Open the timeless_blooms_website folder, and create two new folders. Name one site_files and one development_files.

Copy the asset files that you downloaded from this book's companion site into the development_files folder.

1 prepare your site files

create your site file

There are two types of Flash files that we'll be working with. A FLA file is the working file you create in Flash and do all of your design and development in. FLA files are opened only with Flash. At the other end of the process, a SWF file is the file you export from Flash and post on the Web. The SWF file is your Flash movie and can be opened by browsers, the Flash Player, and some other applications.

Launch Flash, and choose File > New to create your FLA file.

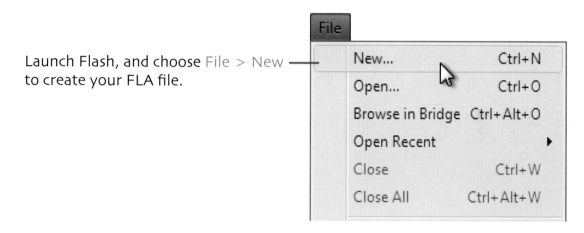

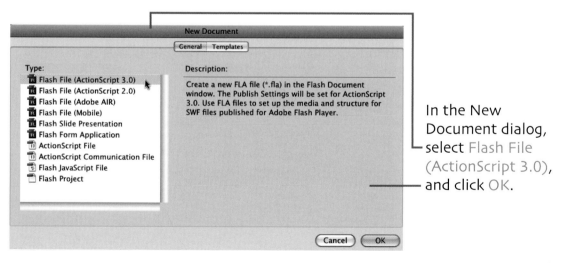

In the New Document dialog, select Flash File (ActionScript 3.0), and click OK.

set document properties

Flash defaults to a canvas size of 550 x 400 pixels with a white background. We can change those settings to fit the needs of our project.

If the Property Inspector is not visible, choose Window > Properties to open it. Note that the panel is labeled Properties, but it is referred to in Adobe Help systems, among Flash users, and in this book as the Property Inspector.

In the Properties section of the Property Inspector, click the Edit button next to the Size property to open the Document Properties dialog.

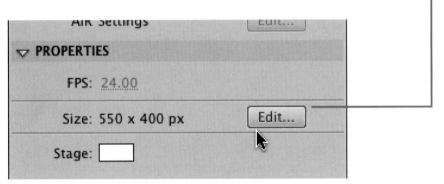

1 In the Document Properties dialog, enter 780 for the width and 600 for the height.

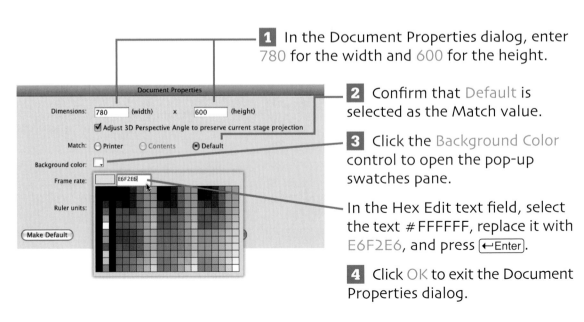

2 Confirm that Default is selected as the Match value.

3 Click the Background Color control to open the pop-up swatches pane.

In the Hex Edit text field, select the text # FFFFFF, replace it with E6F2E6, and press ⏎Enter.

4 Click OK to exit the Document Properties dialog.

1 prepare your site files

save your file

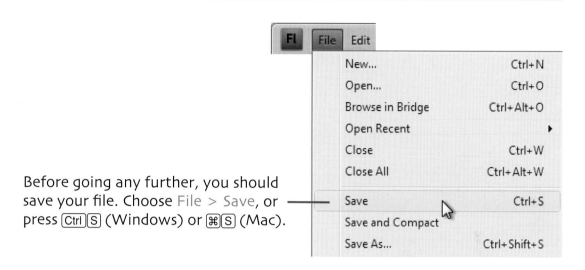

Before going any further, you should save your file. Choose File > Save, or press ⌃S (Windows) or ⌘S (Mac).

In the Save As dialog, navigate to the development_files folder we created earlier. Enter timeless_blooms_site.fla for the file name, and click Save.

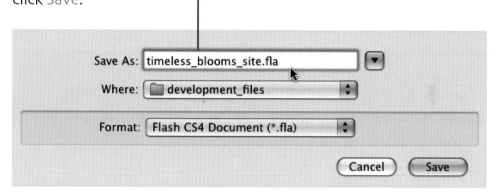

I'll remind you to save your work at the end of each chapter, but you should keep in mind the old edict "Save early and often."

load a workspace

If you are like me, when you install a new application on your computer you like to go exploring, trying different functions to see what they do. In doing so, panels and controls get moved all over the workspace, making for a very cluttered and ineffective work area. You can choose from predefined workspace layouts using the Workspace Switcher in the Application bar.

Flash defaults to the Essentials workspace. Click the Workspace Switcher and choose the Designer workspace, which will work best for our purposes.

You may also gain valuable work area by collapsing panels to icons when not in use. To collapse the panels to icons, click the double-arrow Collapse to Icons control in the Panel title bar.

Additionally, as you become more accustomed to Flash development you will realize that development occurs in stages where some panels are needed and others are not. You can customize and save workspaces to switch for different phases.

1 prepare your site files

save your color scheme

To make applying our color scheme easier and to speed development, we'll first add the colors for our site to the Color Swatches panel, where they can be easily accessed from any of Flash's pop-up swatches panes. (See extra bits on Page 8.)

1 In the Panels Dock click the collapsed Color panel icon to open the Color panel. Click the paintbucket icon to highlight the Fill color selector.

2 To define the dark green color, enter the hex color value 448855 in the Hex value field. Press ⏎Enter.

3 On the right of the panel's title bar, click the Options menu icon, and choose Add Swatch.

Click one of the color controls in the panel to open the swatches pop-up. Notice that our dark green color has been added to the bottom row of swatches.

Repeat steps 1 through 3 to add the other colors to the swatches.

Medium Green: 669966

Dark Purple: 883399

Medium Purple: 994499

Light Purple: BB99CC

Orange: FF8833

Click away from the panel to collapse it back to the dock.

Save your file.

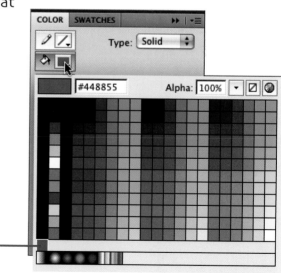

extra bits

save your color scheme p. 7

- Choosing the color scheme for your Web site is an important first step in the design phase of development. Here are a few tips to keep in mind:

  Limit the number of colors used in your design. Too many colors make the design look chaotic and cluttered.

  Pick two or three main colors, and then use different tints of those colors for highlights, backgrounds, etc.

  If your organization has a color logo or a primary graphic for the home page, pull colors from that existing artwork, or choose colors that are complementary.

- You can find color scheme inspiration with the Adobe Kuler panel by choosing Window > Extensions > Kuler. Choose the Browse tab to select color schemes created and shared online by Adobe and other Flash users. Choose the Create tab to create a color scheme based on a color you input.

1 prepare your site files

2. design the layout of your stage

Our first task in Web site development is to design the visual framework within which all of our content will be presented. Think of it as dressing the set of your movie: providing the backdrop, defining different regions, and making it visually attractive. Along the way we'll learn how to use many of Flash's most basic functions. The following are some of the tasks we'll cover:

Create and modify radial gradient fills.

Draw and modify Graphic Primitives.

Use drawing tools to create layout elements.

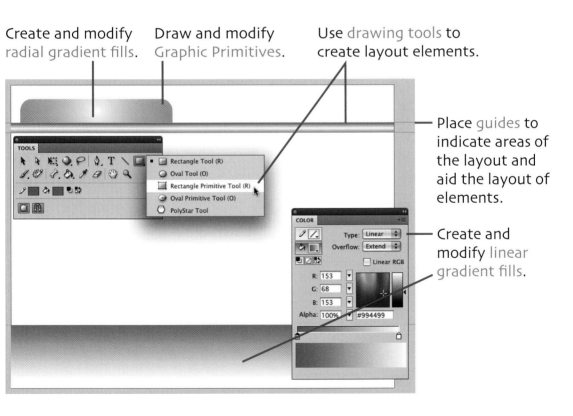

Place guides to indicate areas of the layout and aid the layout of elements.

Create and modify linear gradient fills.

set up guides

Using guides in your file helps you define areas of your Stage and eases placement of objects. Let's add some guides before we begin drawing our background. To ensure correct placement of the guides, we use the Info panel in the expanded state so that it is available for multiple actions.

1 Click the double-arrow Expand Panels control at the top of the Panels Dock to expand panels.

2 In the Align/Info/Transform panel group, click the Info tab to open the Info panel.

3 Choose View > Rulers to turn on rulers along the left and top of the Stage.

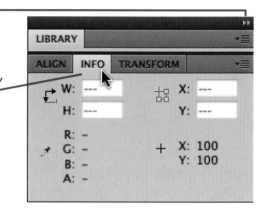

4 Click and drag down a guide from the horizontal (top) ruler. Watch the Info panel; when the cursor location's y value is 75, release the mouse. Drag out two more rules at 95 and 475. Depending on your screen resolution, mouse sensitivity, and current magnification, you might not be able to place the guide at the exact value. Place it as close as possible.

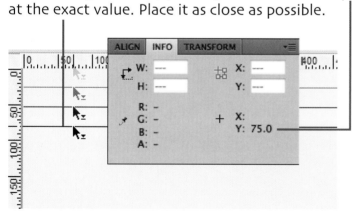

5 Make sure that Snap to Guides is turned on. Choose View > Snapping. In the drop-down menu, look for a check mark next to Snap to Guides. If there's no check mark, click Snap to Guides to turn it on.

6 Adjust the magnification of your view so that the entire stage is visible.

2 design the layout of your stage

draw background

With our Stage divided into different areas, we're ready to begin drawing the objects that will serve as the background for our Web site.

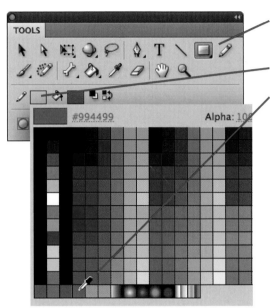

1 In the Tools panel, choose the Rectangle tool.

2 Click the Stroke Color well.

3 In the pop-up swatches pane, move the cursor, now an eyedropper, over our medium purple color and click to select it.

4 Click the Fill color well, and choose white (#FFFFFF) from the swatches.

5 Click to select the Object Drawing option.

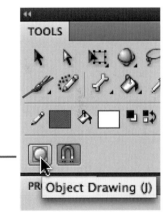

6 Position the cursor at the top-left corner of the Stage. Click and drag out a rectangle to the bottom-right corner of the Stage.

You can make adjustments to the rectangle if size or placement is a little off. In the Property Inspector you can change the values in the width, height, x-position, and y-position text fields. Click and drag on the values to slide the values up or down, or click to select the values and enter correct values manually. Our rectangle should be placed at 0 x-position and 0 y-position and 780 x 600 pixels.

7 Choose Edit > Deselect All to deselect the rectangle.

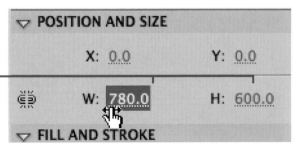

draw background (cont.)

For the next background element make sure the previous rectangle is deselected, the Rectangle tool is selected, and the Object Drawing option is selected.

1 Click the Stroke color well.

2 In the pop-up swatches pane, click the None button near the top-right corner of the pop-up.

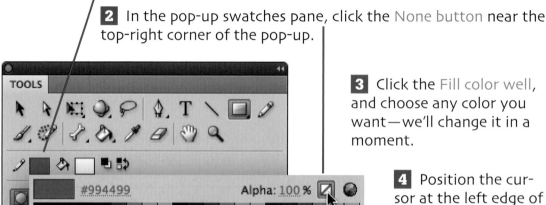

3 Click the Fill color well, and choose any color you want—we'll change it in a moment.

4 Position the cursor at the left edge of the Stage on top of the guide you placed at 75. Click and drag out a rectangle to the right edge of the Stage and down to the guide at 95.

If necessary, use the Property Inspector to set the dimension and position values to 780 x 20 and 0,75 for the x and y text.

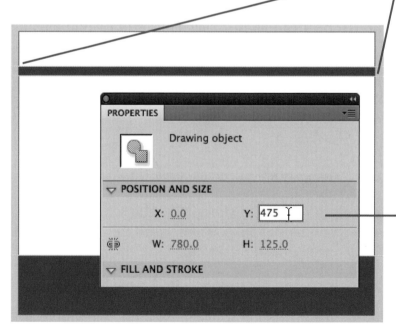

5 Draw another rectangle with these values: 780 x 125 and 0,475.

6 Choose Edit > Deselect All to deselect the rectangle.

2 design the layout of your stage

draw object primitives

Our final background element will be a special object known as a Rectangle Primitive. Primitive objects are special object shapes that allow you to adjust characteristics in the Property Inspector. This lets you precisely control the size, corner radius, and other properties of the shape at any time after you have created it without having to redraw it from scratch.

We'll use the corner radius feature of Rectangle Primitives to create a tabbed appearance in our layout.

1 In the Tools panel press and hold the Rectangle tool. From the drop-down menu select the Rectangle Primitive tool.

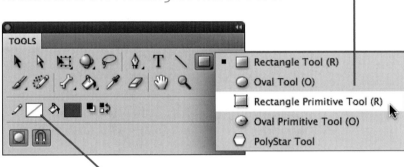

2 Click the Stroke color well and choose our medium purple color.

3 Position the cursor about 20 pixels from the left edge of the Stage on top of the guide you placed at 75.

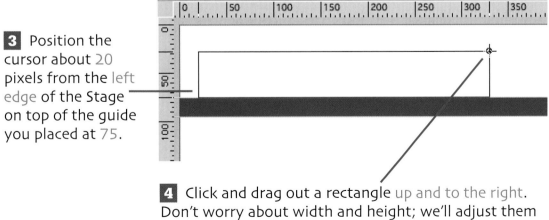

4 Click and drag out a rectangle up and to the right. Don't worry about width and height; we'll adjust them in a later chapter.

edit primitives

Rectangle Primitive corners are changed by clicking and dragging the corner Radius Handles or by changing values in the Corner Radius controls in the Property Inspector. We'll do both.

1 Choose the Selection tool from the Tools panel.

2 Click one of the four Radius Handles on the Rectangle Primitive and drag either direction along the rectangle's edge. A guide appears showing the radius you are creating.

3 Release when you have a nicely rounded corner.

Note that all four corners of the Rectangle Primitive reflect the new radius you dragged out.

To create a tabbed appearance we only want rounded corners at the top left and right.

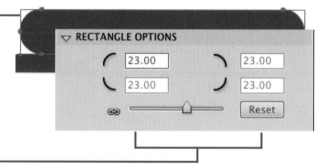

In the Property Inspector note that the value in the first Corner Radius control has changed and that the other three controls are disabled (grayed out).

4 Click the Lock icon to unlock the relationship between the four corners, allowing each corner to be edited separately.

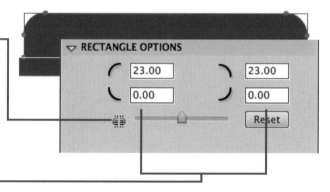

5 Change the bottom left and right values to 0 to bring them back to square corners.

add gradient fills

Next we'll add gradient fills, in which colors gradually blend from one into another, to give our design a sense of depth.

Choose the Selection tool from the Tools panel, and click the rectangle between the guides at 75 and 95 to select it. Press [Shift] and click the rectangle you drew below the guide at 475 and the Rectangle Primitive to add them to the selection.

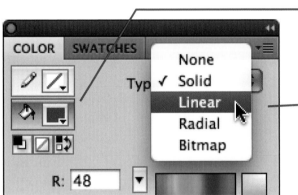

With the three rectangles selected, in the Color panel click the Fill color well.

Click the Type drop-down menu (also referred to as Fill Style in the tool tip), and select Linear. The fill of the rectangles will change to a gradient.

You'll see a new control on the panel—a gradient definition bar with pointers below the bar indicating each color in the gradient.

Double-click the pointer on the left end of the gradient definition bar to open the swatches pop-up. Choose our medium purple color.

Now the rectangles have purple-to-white gradient fills, but they're not the way we want. We'll change them next.

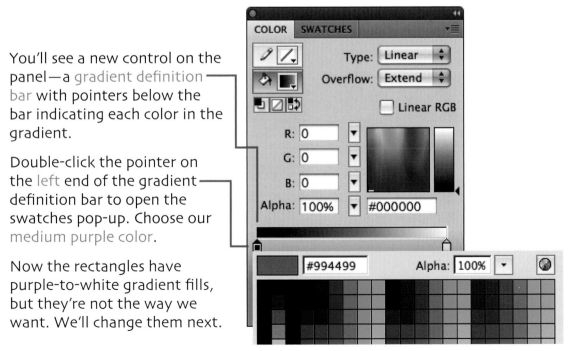

edit gradient fills

With the Selection tool, click outside the Stage to deselect the three rectangles.

Select View > Guides > Show Guides to turn off guides, making our object edges easier to see.

Click to select the rectangle at the bottom of the stage.

In the Tools panel press and hold the Free Transform tool. From the drop-down menu choose the Gradient Transform tool.

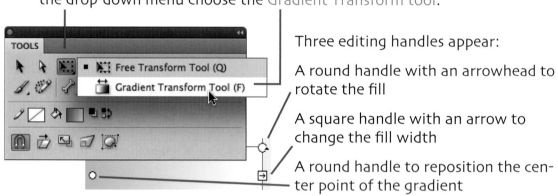

Three editing handles appear:

A round handle with an arrowhead to rotate the fill

A square handle with an arrow to change the fill width

A round handle to reposition the center point of the gradient

Click and drag the round rotation handle down and toward the center to rotate the fill 90°.

Press (Shift) to snap rotation to 45° increments.

If necessary, adjust your view to see the square fill width handle. Click and drag the handle to the bottom edge of the rectangle.

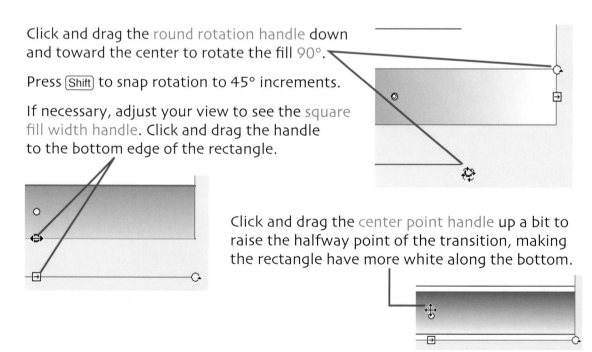

Click and drag the center point handle up a bit to raise the halfway point of the transition, making the rectangle have more white along the bottom.

With the Gradient Transform tool still selected, click to select the smaller rectangle near the top of the Stage.

The three editing handles appear.

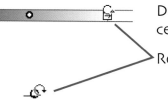

Drag the square fill width handle toward the center point, stopping around 100 pixels away.

Rotate the fill 90°.

Zooming in on the rectangle and the gradient transform handles will allow us to make more exact adjustments to the gradient in the coming steps. Press and hold Ctrl Spacebar (Windows) or Spacebar ⌘ (Mac) to temporarily change the cursor to the Magnify tool. Click and drag out a rectangle that surrounds the gradient center point and the square fill width handle. Release to zoom the view.

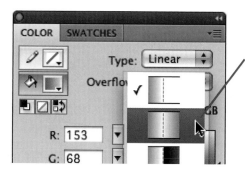

In the Color panel, click the Overflow drop-down menu and choose the second entry, which reflects a black-to-white-to-black gradient. This makes the fill wrap to create a 3D effect. Overflow defines how the fill appears outside the boundaries of the gradient fill width. Our selection reflects the gradient across the fill width's edge.

Click and drag the square fill width handle toward the center point until the two fill guides are about halfway between the center point and the edge of the rectangle.

Click and drag the center point handle to raise the halfway point of the transition, creating the 3D appearance.

edit gradient fills (cont.)

Our final step in working with the gradient fills of the background objects is to apply and edit a Radial Gradient fill in the Rectangle Primitive.

Select View > Magnification > 100% to bring the Rectangle Primitive into view, choose the Selection tool from the Tools panel, and click to select the Rectangle Primitive.

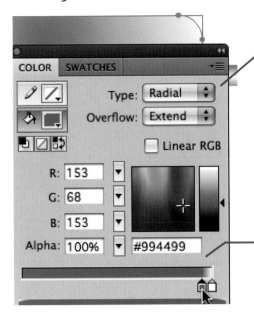

In the Color panel, click the Type drop-down menu, and select Radial.

The fill changes to a Radial Gradient.

The gradient, with purple in the middle and white at the edges, is the opposite of what we want. We can redefine it in the Color panel.

On the gradient definition bar click and drag the purple-filled pointer to the right, stopping when you near the white pointer.

Now drag the white pointer to the left as far as it will go.

Finally, drag the purple pointer the remainder of the way to the right.

With the purple pointer still selected, change the Alpha value to 60%, making the purple color semitransparent against the white background and giving the color a lighter appearance.

That completes our work on the rectangles.

3. add and style text

With the graphic elements of the background in place, we can now add some text. We begin by adding and manipulating static text. (In later chapters we'll do more advanced things with text.) In this chapter we'll do the following:

Add and manipulate fixed-width text boxes.

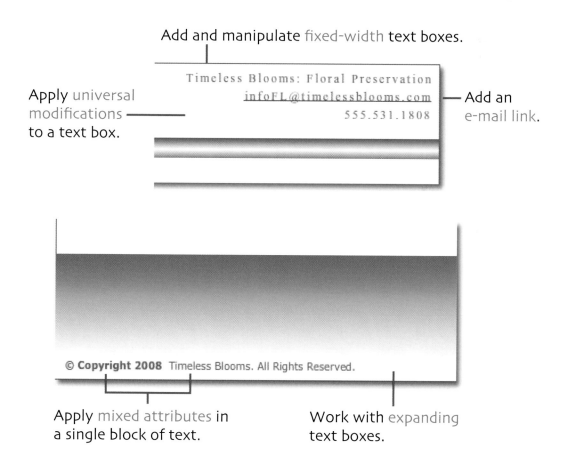

Apply universal modifications to a text box.

Timeless Blooms: Floral Preservation
infoFL@timelessblooms.com
555.531.1808

Add an e-mail link.

© Copyright 2008 Timeless Blooms. All Rights Reserved.

Apply mixed attributes in a single block of text.

Work with expanding text boxes.

add a single line of text

For our first simple text exercise we'll add company and copyright information to the layout.

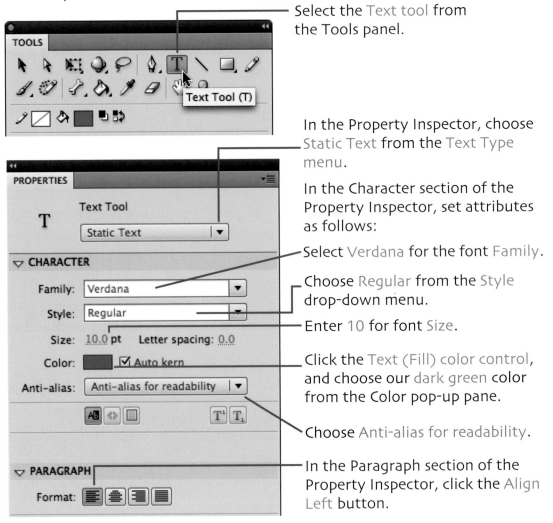

Select the Text tool from the Tools panel.

In the Property Inspector, choose Static Text from the Text Type menu.

In the Character section of the Property Inspector, set attributes as follows:

Select Verdana for the font Family.

Choose Regular from the Style drop-down menu.

Enter 10 for font Size.

Click the Text (Fill) color control, and choose our dark green color from the Color pop-up pane.

Choose Anti-alias for readability.

In the Paragraph section of the Property Inspector, click the Align Left button.

Click the Text tool near the bottom-left corner of the Stage. An empty text box with a blinking insertion point appears. The round Resize handle denotes that the text box does not have a fixed width and will expand horizontally to hold all the text entered.

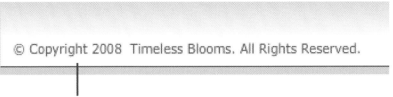

© Copyright 2008 Timeless Blooms. All Rights Reserved.

Type © Copyright 2008 Timeless Blooms. All Rights Reserved.

To enter the copyright symbol (©), press and hold Option and type G (Mac) or press and hold Alt and type 0169 on the number pad (Windows). (Note that you cannot enter the numbers from the main keyboard on Windows.) On some Windows laptops, you may have to hold the Fn key to enter the numbers.

Click on the Stage to close the text box.

Let's change the attributes of some of the text in this text box to add emphasis to the copyright notice.

With the Text tool still selected, click inside the text box to edit the text inside.

To select the text © Copyright 2008, click to the left of the copyright symbol and drag past the 8.

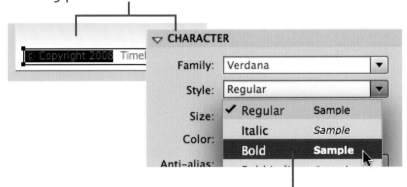

With the text now selected, in the Character section of the Property Inspector click the Style drop-down menu and choose Bold.

3 add and style text

fixed-width text

Click on the Stage to close and deselect the text box. In the Property Inspector, change the font Family to Times New Roman, Style to Regular, and the Size to 12.

1 With the Text tool selected, move the cursor to a point near the top of the Stage and aligned approximately with the 570 pixels mark on the horizontal ruler.

2 Click and drag out a text box, stopping near the 700 pixels mark.

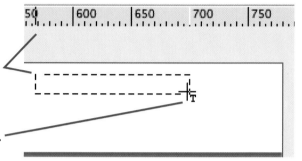

An empty text box appears.

The square Resize handle denotes that the box has a fixed width, meaning text will wrap onto new lines rather than stay on one line and stretch the text box.

3 Enter Timeless Blooms: Floral Preservation.

Because the text box is not wide enough, the last word will wrap to the next line.

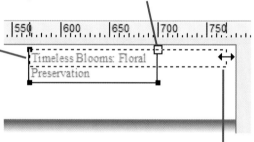

4 Click and drag the Resize handle to about the 770 pixels mark. Now the text fits on one line.

5 Press (↵Enter), and type infoFL@timelessblooms.com.

6 Press (↵Enter), and type 555.531.1808.

7 Choose the Selection tool from the Tools panel to close the text box.

change a text box

You can make universal changes to all of the text in a text box by selecting the box and making changes in the Property Inspector.

If the text box is not still selected, click it with the Selection tool.

Click the Align Right button in the Paragraph section of the Property Inspector.

To spread out the lines of text, change the Line Spacing value to 5.

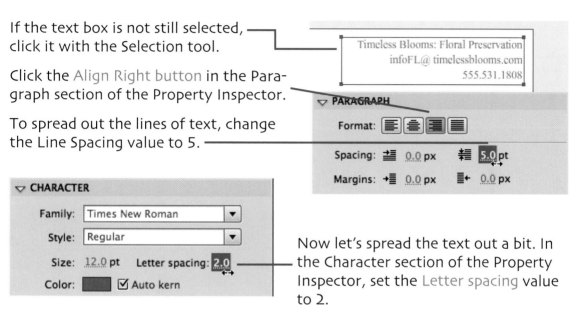

Now let's spread the text out a bit. In the Character section of the Property Inspector, set the Letter spacing value to 2.

The last step caused the text on the first line to wrap again. Double-click the text box and drag out the Resize handle until the text fits on the first line again.

Now the text is drawing off the edge of the Stage! Move the cursor over the text container's bounding box until it changes to a pointer, and reposition the text box so that all the text appears on the Stage.

add an e-mail link

We want contacting Timeless Blooms to be convenient for viewers of the Web site. Let's add a link to the e-mail address that will automatically launch a new message in the viewer's e-mail application.

Select the text infoFL@timelessblooms.com.

Choose Edit > Copy to copy the e-mail address to the clipboard.

With the text still highlighted, go to the Property Inspector's Options section and type mailto: in the Link field and then paste the e-mail address into the field. Make sure there is no space between the colon and the pasted address.

Press ⏎Enter to set the URL attribute.

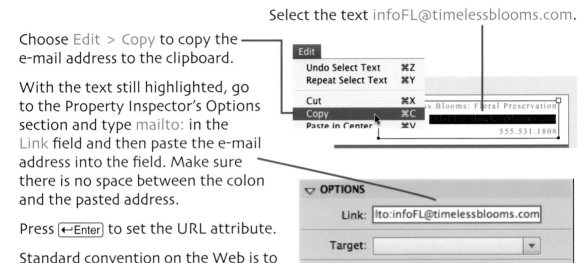

Standard convention on the Web is to underline clickable text. A line appears under the e-mail address, but this is only a visual clue inside the Flash authoring environment; it won't be visible in the exported movie.

Flash doesn't provide an Underline style for text, so we'll create our own.

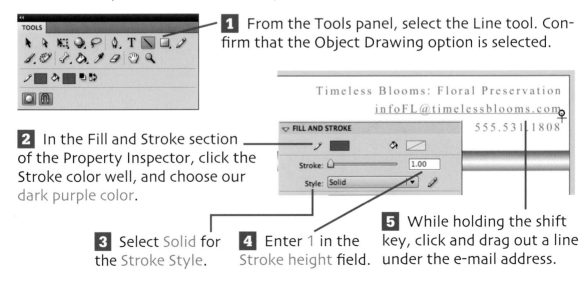

1 From the Tools panel, select the Line tool. Confirm that the Object Drawing option is selected.

2 In the Fill and Stroke section of the Property Inspector, click the Stroke color well, and choose our dark purple color.

3 Select Solid for the Stroke Style.

4 Enter 1 in the Stroke height field.

5 While holding the shift key, click and drag out a line under the e-mail address.

3 add and style text

4. work with imported objects

So far we've used Tools included in the Flash application to create different types of objects for our layout. In this chapter, you'll learn how to incorporate layout elements created in other graphics applications.

You'll also learn to keep the elements in our project organized, allowing for increased ease of development tasks. Here are some of the tasks we'll cover:

Import and transform vector artwork.

Apply transformations to objects without distorting corners.

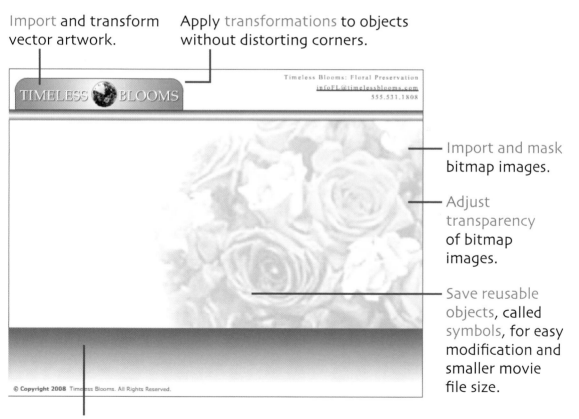

Import and mask bitmap images.

Adjust transparency of bitmap images.

Save reusable objects, called symbols, for easy modification and smaller movie file size.

Create layers to organize your file.

reusable graphics

Since the framework that we've created will serve as the background of our Web site, we can reuse what we've drawn multiple times, for each page of our site. To do that, we need to convert the elements into one reusable symbol. When a symbol is used on the Stage, it's called an instance. (See extra bits on page 40.)

To select all the elements of the framework, choose Edit > Select All, or press Ctrl A (Windows) or ⌘ A (Mac).

Edit	
Undo Line	Ctrl+Z
Repeat Line	Ctrl+Y
Cut	Ctrl+X
Copy	Ctrl+C
Paste in Center	Ctrl+V
Paste in Place	Ctrl+Shift+V
Paste Special...	
Clear	Backspace
Duplicate	Ctrl+D
Select All	Ctrl+A
Deselect All	Ctrl+Shift+A
Find and Replace	Ctrl+F
Find Next	F3

Modify	
Document...	⌘J
Convert to Symbol...	F8
Break Apart	⌘B

Choose Modify > Convert to Symbol, or press F8.

In the Convert to Symbol dialog, name the symbol gr_siteFramework. The gr_ signifies the symbol type. As we create more symbols we'll use similar naming and abbreviation schemes to help us keep our symbols straight.

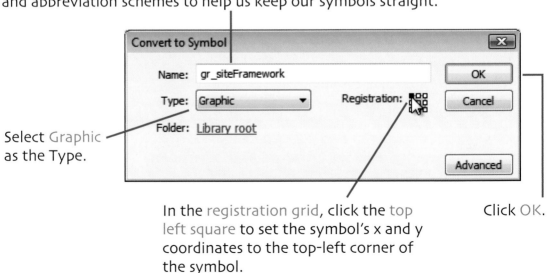

Select Graphic as the Type.

In the registration grid, click the top left square to set the symbol's x and y coordinates to the top-left corner of the symbol.

Click OK.

4 work with imported objects

The rectangles and text that we created so far have now been moved into the
gr_siteFramework symbol, and an instance of that symbol has replaced them on
the Stage.

In the Color/Swatches panel group in the Panels Dock,
click to the right of the tabs to collapse the panel group
thus expanding the view of the Library panel.

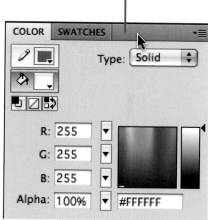

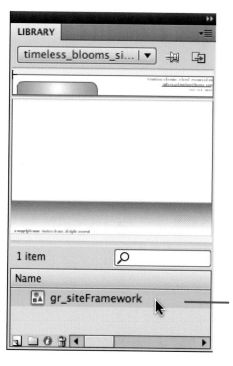

In the Library panel, note the addition of
your gr_siteFramework symbol.

Notice in the Property Inspector
that new controls have appeared,
reflecting the selection of the
symbol instance.

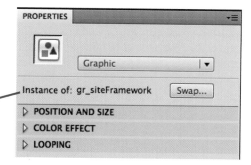

import vector art

Sometimes you'll need to include artwork that has been created in another application or file format. Here we're going to import logo artwork that's been provided in an Adobe Fireworks PNG file that contains vectors (editable paths) and bitmap objects (images).

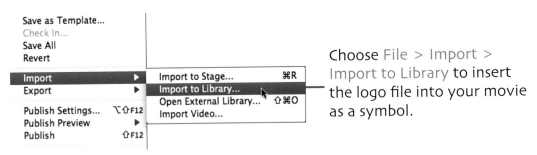

Choose File > Import > Import to Library to insert the logo file into your movie as a symbol.

In the Import to Library dialog, locate the file logo.png, which you downloaded from this book's companion Web site and copied into the site's development_files folder. Select the file, and click Open (Windows) or Import to Library (Mac).

In the Import Fireworks Document dialog that appears, set the following options:

Import: Page 1

Into: Current frame as movie clip

Objects: Keep all paths editable

Text: Either choice will work in this case because all the text in the logo has been converted to vector paths to avoid font issues.

Do not check the Import as a single flattened bitmap check box.

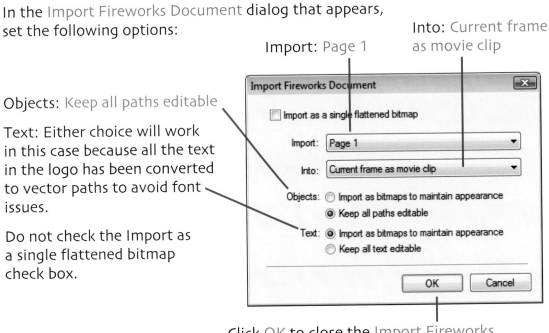

Click OK to close the Import Fireworks Document dialog.

Now the logo has been added to the Library.

4 work with imported objects

organize symbols

In the Library panel, you'll see two new listings—a graphic symbol named logo.png and a folder named Fireworks Objects that contains the objects that make up the logo. Let's take a moment to begin organizing our symbols, which will save us time and headaches later.

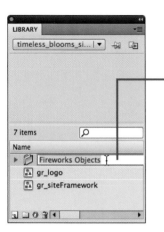

Double-click the symbol name logo.png in the Library panel to select the text. Be sure you double-click the text, not the icon. Change it to gr_logo, and press ⏎Enter.

Double-click the folder name to select the text Fireworks Objects. Enter logo parts, and press ⏎Enter.

Click to select the symbol gr_logo. Drag the symbol onto the logo parts folder and release.

Click the small triangle next to the logo parts folder icon to expand the folder view, and verify that the symbol is in the folder along with the folders containing objects that make up the symbol gr_logo.

Click in the empty area of the Library panel to deselect the gr_logo symbol.

Click the New Folder button at the bottom of the Library panel to add a new folder to the list. Name the folder framework parts.

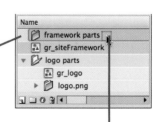

Drag the symbol gr_siteFramework into the new folder.

symbol-editing mode

Once a symbol is created we'll often want to "get at" the elements inside for further editing. To do this we enter symbol-editing mode. (See extra bits on page 40.) There are two styles of symbol-editing mode. Default Edit mode opens the symbol in its own window with no other elements visible. Edit in Place lets you edit the symbol in the location at which an instance is placed and allows you to see the other objects on the Stage.

There are also multiple ways to enter symbol-editing mode:

For default editing mode:

- Double-click the symbol preview or symbol icon in the Library panel.

- Select an instance on the Stage and choose Edit > Edit Symbols or Edit > Edit Selected.

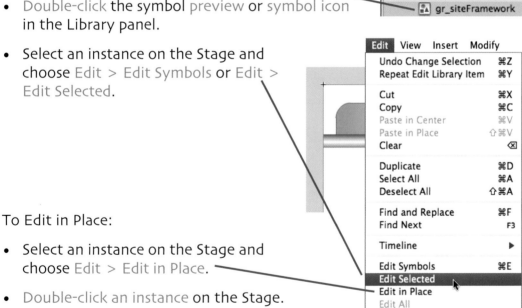

To Edit in Place:

- Select an instance on the Stage and choose Edit > Edit in Place.

- Double-click an instance on the Stage.

Edit in Place is our preferred manner because it allows you to edit the symbol in context with the rest of the Stage. When you're instructed to double-click a symbol or instance or to enter symbol-editing mode, always choose the Edit in Place mode, unless instructed otherwise.

Next, let's add a logo to the gr_siteFramework symbol.

transform objects

Objects on your Stage, even symbols, can have different transformations applied to them. Transformations such as Scale, Rotate, and Skew are applied with the Free Transform tool. (See extra bits on page 40.)

With the Selection tool selected, double-click the gr_siteFramework instance on the Stage to invoke symbol-editing mode.

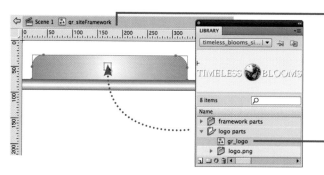

In the Edit Bar, confirm that you're in symbol-editing mode.

In the Library panel, open the logo parts folder, select the symbol gr_logo, and drag it onto the Stage over the center of the Rectangle Primitive.

Depending on how you drew the Rectangle Primitive, it will either be larger or smaller than we want, so we'll scale it to fit nicely around the logo.

In the Tools panel, choose the Free Transform tool.

Click to select the Rectangle Primitive. Be careful to select the background tab and not the logo.

Eight transformation handles appear around the rectangle's bounding box. The four corner handles scale width and height together and the four side handles stretch the object.

Click and drag the transformation handles as necessary to make the Rectangle Primitive fit around the logo, giving the logo a nice background. Press and hold Shift to scale an object proportionally. Press and hold Option (Mac) or Alt

(Windows) to transform the object in a single direction instead of from the center.

Choose the Selection tool to set the transformation.

set 9-slice scaling

Notice that scaling the Rectangle Primitive distorted the rounded corners. We can avoid that by using 9-slice scaling, a technique that defines nine areas of an object, four of which (the corners) are not changed when an object is scaled or stretched.

With the Rectangle Primitive still selected, choose Modify > Transform > Remove Transform to return the Rectangle Primitive to its original shape. If necessary, use the arrow keys to nudge the rectangle back to its original position.

Choose Modify > Convert to Symbol, or press F8.

In the Convert to Symbol dialog, name the symbol mc_logoTab.

Select Movie Clip as the Type. Even though we're only using the rectangle as a graphic element, the 9-slice scaling feature only works on Movie Clip symbols.

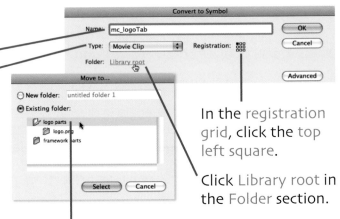

In the registration grid, click the top left square.

Click Library root in the Folder section.

In the Move to... dialog, choose Existing folder, select logo parts, and click Select.

In the Convert to Symbol dialog, click Advanced to expand the dialog and reveal more controls.

Choose Enable guides for 9-slice scaling.

Click OK.

On the Stage, notice that the symbol instance is now on top of the logo. Choose Modify > Arrange > Send Backward to move the instance behind the logo.

4 work with imported objects

With the Selection tool selected, double-click the mc_logoTab instance on the Stage to invoke symbol-editing mode.

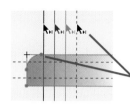

The dashed lines are the slice guides that we can adjust to define the four areas that will not stretch when transformed.

Move the cursor over the left vertical guide until the cursor changes. Click and drag the guide left until it is just inside the Radius Handle.

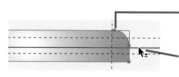

Click and drag the right vertical guide to the right until it is just inside the Radius Handle.

Click and drag the top horizontal guide until it is just below the side Radius Handles.

You've now defined the top-right and -left corners as areas that will not stretch.

We don't need to worry about the bottom corners because they're not affected by a transformation.

In the Edit Bar, click gr_siteFramework to exit symbol-editing mode on mc_logoTab and return to editing gr_siteFramework.

With the Free Transform tool, click to select the mc_logoTab instance.

As you did before, click and drag the transformation handles as necessary to make the rectangle fit around the logo, giving the logo a nice background.

Click outide the instance's bounding box to set the transformation.

Choose the Selection tool.

Note that the two rounded corners have maintained their original appearance.

If necessary, use the arrow keys to nudge the instance to align it with the logo or the gradient rectangle below it.

object hierarchies

We use various constructs like scenes, frames, layers, symbols, and groups as containers to organize files. Editing symbols and groups can get confusing because oftentimes groups are placed inside other groups that are inside symbols inside other symbols. Confused yet? Imagine what it's like to edit them! The keys to success are the Edit Bar and the Property Inspector. Let's try them out.

In the Edit Bar confirm you're still in symbol-editing mode on the gr_siteFramework symbol. With the Selection tool, select the gr_logo instance and choose View > Magnification > 400% to zoom way in.

1 Double-click on the clock. The Edit Bar shows you're editing three levels in—Scene 1 > gr_siteFramework > gr_logo.

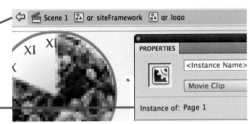

2 Click to select the clock. The Property Inspector shows that an instance of symbol Page 1 is selected.

3 Double-click the clock again. The Edit Bar shows you're one level further in.

4 Click away from the clock to deselect any objects, then select the clock again. The Property Inspector shows the clock is actually a group.

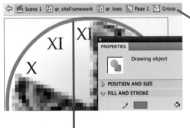

5 Double-click the clock group. The Edit Bar reflects the new editing level, Scene 1 > gr_site-Framework > gr_logo > Page 1 > Group.

6 We want to select the circle with a pink stroke that makes up the clock's frame. Zoom to 800%.

7 Choose Edit > Deselect All, then click on the very edge of the pink frame. It might take a couple of tries to select the circle and not the bouquet image.

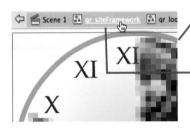

8 Once selected, click the Stroke color well in the Property Inspector and choose our orange color.

With the edit made we can return to editing the gr_siteFramework symbol by clicking gr_siteFramework in the Edit Bar.

Return the view to 100%.

4 work with imported objects

organize with layers

Layers, as we outlined before, are a great organizational tool. They control the stacking order of objects in a Timeline. We're going to create a new layer above the current one and move our logo there. But first let's modify our workspace.

We'll work away from the panels in the Panels Dock for a bit, so let's take this opportunity to maximize our work area by collapsing the Panels Dock to the Icons configuration.

Click the double arrow at the top of the Panels Dock to collapse it.

Now let's begin working with layers. We'll rename the current layer to reflect what it contains. Be certain that you are in the gr_siteFramework symbol.

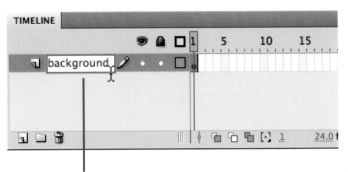

In the Layers column of the Timeline, double-click the text Layer 1 to select it. Enter background for the layer name, and press ⏎Enter.

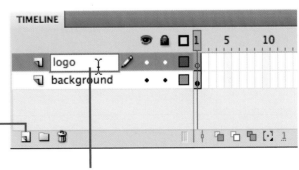

1 Click the New Layer button at the bottom of the Layers column. A new layer appears in the layers list.

2 Double-click the layer name, and change it to logo.

move between layers

Now we want to move the symbol gr_logo from the background layer to the new layer that we've created to hold it. Moving objects from one layer to another in Flash works differently than in most drawing applications. Here's how it's done.

With the Selection tool, click to select the instance of the symbol gr_logo on the background layer.

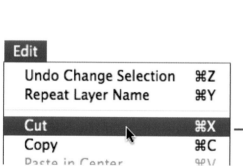

— Choose Edit > Cut to move the gr_logo instance from the background layer to the clipboard.

In the Timeline, click the logo layer to make it the active layer.

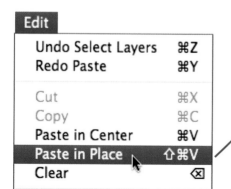

Choose Edit > Paste in Place to paste the Logo instance into the exact same location, just on the different layer.

4 work with imported objects

import bitmap image

With the logo sized and placed, let's add some interest to the main area of our layout.

In the Edit Bar confirm that you are still in symbol-editing mode.

1 In the Timeline, add a new layer.

2 Name the layer bouquet.

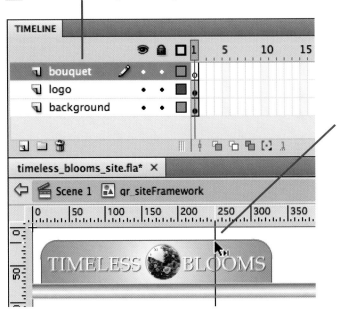

3 Choose View > Guides > Show Guides to turn them on.

From the vertical ruler, drag out a guide and place it approximately halfway between the bouquet/clock in the logo and the right edge of the Rectangle Primitive.

4 With the bouquet layer still selected, choose File > Import > Import to Stage. In the Import dialog, navigate to the development_files folder. Select the bouquet_large.jpg file, and click Import (Mac) or Open (Windows).

The bouquet image is placed on the stage.

5 With the Selection tool, drag the image into place, aligning the left edge with the vertical guide and the top edge with the top of the Stage.

add masking layer

The bouquet image is too big and covers up too much of the layout. We only want part of the bouquet image to display, so we'll use a layer mask to hide the unwanted parts.

1 In the Timeline, click in the Eye column to the right of the layer name bouquet to temporarily hide the image.

2 Add a new layer, and name it bouquet mask.

3 Select the Rectangle tool.

4 Set the Stroke color well to none.

5 Set the Fill color well to black.

6 Place the cursor over the intersection of the horizontal guide at 95 and the vertical guide aligned with the left edge of the image.

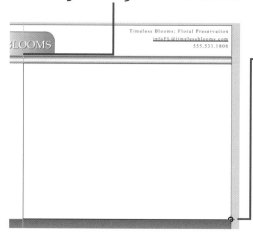

7 Click and drag the box down and to the right. The Y axis guide should read 475 for the bottom of the box.

8 Click the red X in the Eye column on the bouquet layer to make the image visible again.

9 Right-click (Windows) or Control -click (Mac) the layer bouquet mask. Choose Mask from the drop-down menu.

Note that the bouquet and bouquet_ mask layers are locked. This is required for the mask to display correctly.

The visible area of the image is now cropped within the confines of the masking rectangle.

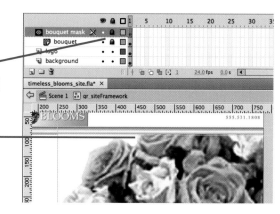

edit masked objects

Finally, for the layout we want to fade the bouquet image so that it is very light behind the content we'll be adding later.

To edit a masked object, you must temporarily turn the masking off by unlocking the two layers that make up the mask.

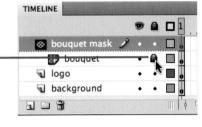

1 In the Timeline, click the Lock icons in the bouquet mask and bouquet layers.

The full bouquet image and the black rectangle are now visible on the Stage.

To adjust transparency, or Alpha, of an object, it must be converted to a symbol.

2 With the Selection tool, click to select the bouquet image.

3 Choose Modify > Convert to Symbol, or press F8 . In the Convert to Symbol dialog, name the symbol gr_bouquetImage and select Graphic as the Type. Click Library root and place the new symbol in the framework parts folder. Click Select and then click OK in the Convert to Symbol dialog.

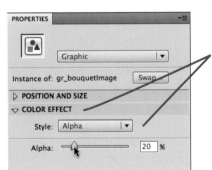

4 In the Property Inspector, open the Color Effect section. Click the Style menu, and select Alpha. Set the Alpha value to 20%.

The bitmap image is faded the way we want.

5 To turn masking back on, click in the Lock column of the bouquet mask and bouquet layers.

In the Edit Bar click Scene 1 to exit symbol-editing mode.

That's it! Our layout framework is now complete.

4 work with imported objects   **39**

extra bits

reusable graphics p. 26

- Using symbols in Flash provides two main benefits: reduced file size and ease of editing.

  When you create a symbol and place instances of that symbol on the Stage, your movie's file size is reduced because no matter how many times you use it, the code required to define it is only included in the file once. Each instance just points to the symbol and describes any modifications to that symbol, such as transparency or size.

  Modifying work later is also much easier. Imagine that you've placed 100 blue squares (not instances of a blue square symbol) throughout your movie, and then you decide to change the color. You have to find and change all 100 squares. But if you made a symbol of a blue square and placed 100 instances, you only have to change the symbol, and the 100 instances are updated automatically.

symbol-editing mode p. 30

- When you have an object on the Stage that is a container for other objects (groups, symbols, and text boxes), you can just double-click it to "get inside" and edit the contents.

- To exit the editing mode of the container, you can double-click outside the bounds of the container or use the Edit bar.

transform objects p. 31

- When you're scaling vector objects (those drawn in Flash or imported from Illustrator or Fireworks, as in the logo file.) you can increase or decrease the size without any negative effects. However, if you're working with a bitmap image, you'll want to avoid enlarging it. An enlarged bitmap has to be resampled and can become distorted or fuzzy. It's best to open the image in an image editor such as Adobe Photoshop and scale it to the size you need.

5. use the timelin
organize your site

As you've probably guessed, the Timeline is used for animation in your Flash movie. But it also serves other purposes.

A frame can represent not only a fluid moment in an animation as an object slides across the Stage, but also a static point to which we navigate within our movie. In Flash development we use frames for animation, as reference points, and as organizational tools to ease development.

In this chapter, we learn the basics of working with different types of frames, naming frames for easy reference, and controlling frame playback. We'll learn to:

Add frame labels   Insert keyframes

Add frames to the Timeline

Use outlines and highlights to distinguish selections

Import Adobe Illustrator files

Control the Timeline with ActionScript

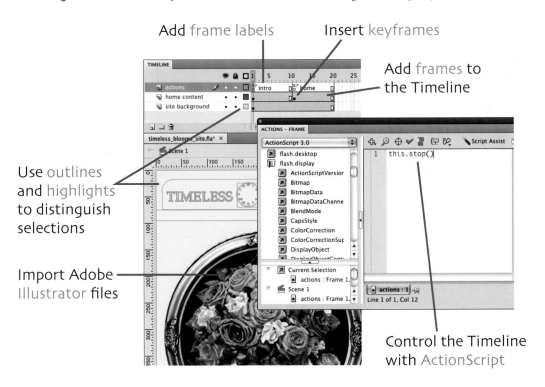

llustrator import

We've established the framework for our design. Now it's time to work on the Home section of the site. First, let's add some content from an Adobe Illustrator file. Flash offers many options for importing layers and objects in the file, and we'll make selections based on how we'll use the different elements in our project.

Turn off guides by selecting View > Guides > Show Guides or pressing Ctrl ; (Windows) or ⌘ ; (Mac).

1 In the Timeline, rename the existing layer site background.

2 Add a new layer and leave the default name Layer 2 it will be changed later.

3 Add another layer named actions.

4 Click Layer 2 to make it the active layer.

5 Choose File > Import > Import to Stage. In the Import dialog, navigate to the development_files folder. Select the file home graphic.ai, and click Import.

The Import "home graphic.ai" to Stage dialog that appears provides import options that we can customize.

The Object Options section of the dialog displays all of the different layers and objects that are in the Illustrator file.

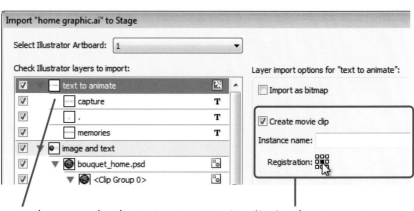

Select the text to animate layer and select Create Movie Clip in the Layer Import Options section of the dialog. Leave the Instance Name value empty. In the Registration control, click the center square. The layer contains three text blocks to be used in an animation. Importing them into a Movie Clip will save us time later.

Shift-click to select the three text objects. Set them to import as Editable Text.

Select the layer image and text. Choose Create Movie Clip.

Select bouquet_home.psd and choose Import as Bitmap to collapse the subitems into one image.

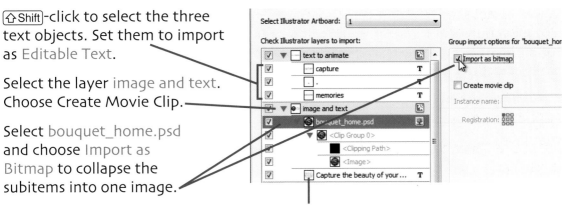

Set the line of text that begins "Capture the beauty of…" to Import as Vector Outlines.

Uncheck the box next to the layer mock-up from creative so it won't be imported.

Set Convert Layers To to Single Flash Layer.

Uncheck the remaining options, and click OK.

The selected elements of the Illustrator file are placed on the Stage. With the Selection tool, drag the graphics into place.

In the Timeline, note the layer name has changed to match the filename we imported. Change it to home content.

In the Panels Dock, click the Library icon to expand it. In the Library panel, a folder named home graphic.ai is created. Rename the folder home parts.

As a clean-up action, drag bouquet_large.jpg into the framework parts folder. Click anywhere away from the Library to close the panel.

I won't instruct you to organize symbols throughout the rest of this book; however, keep in mind the techniques covered earlier.

5 use the timeline to organize your site 43

outlines & highlights

You may have noticed that it is sometimes difficult to identify what objects you have selected or that it is difficult to examine an object because of the surrounding objects. Two related features, Outline Display and Colored Highlights, address those difficulties.

In the Layers column of the Timeline, clicking the color icon at the right turns the objects in that layer to Outline Display.

In the layer site background click the icon from the bottom layer.

Objects in the gr_siteFramework instance on the layer now display as outlines and the outline color matches the color of the icon for that layer.

Click the icon again to turn Outline Display off.

You can also use the colors for Outline Mode to highlight selected objects.

Choose Edit > Preferences (Windows) or Flash > Preferences (Mac) to open the Preferences dialog.

In the Category List, select General.

Change the Highlight Color setting to Use Layer Color. Click OK.

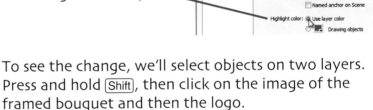

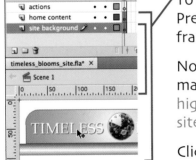

To see the change, we'll select objects on two layers. Press and hold (Shift), then click on the image of the framed bouquet and then the logo.

Note that the highlight color for the bouquet object matches the color for the home content layer and the highlight color on the framework symbol matches the site background layer.

Click the Pasteboard outside the Stage to deselect the objects.

frames & keyframes

Currently we have only one frame in our movie. The frames that you see in the Timeline now are available frames, but they're not yet defined. We'll define more frames to help us organize our movie and prepare it for adding animations (which we'll do in the next chapter). (See extra bits on Page 51.)

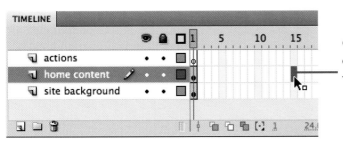

In the Timeline for the home content layer, click the empty cell beneath the 15 marker in the Timeline Header.

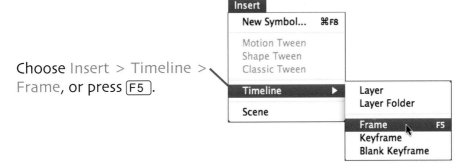

Choose Insert > Timeline > Frame, or press F5.

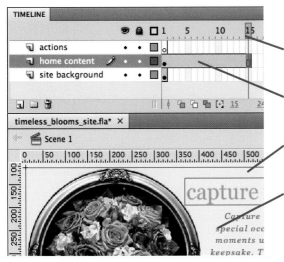

Notice four things:

The Playhead has moved to display Frame 15.

Flash has automatically created frames 2 through 14.

Our gr_siteFramework symbol is not visible.

The contents of the layer's keyframe at Frame 1 are displayed now in Frame 15.

frames & keyframes (cont.)

We have no Framework because Frame 15 has not been defined for the site background layer. Add the frame now, repeating the steps you took to create the frame for the home content layer.

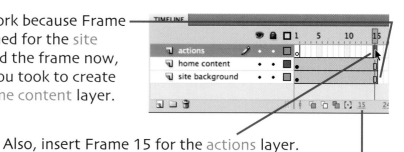

Also, insert Frame 15 for the actions layer.

Note the Current Frame display beneath the Timeline in case you have difficulty determining what frame you're in.

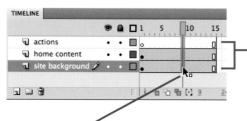

We now have 15 frames in each of our layers. Let's add five more frames to all the layers at once.

In the actions layer, click to select one of the frames (it doesn't matter which one). Press and hold Shift and click the same frame number in the site background layer, selecting the frame in all three layers. Choose Insert > Timeline > Frame five times, or press F5 five times.

Now we're going to add keyframes, which will let us change content from one point in the Timeline to another.

Click Frame 11 in the home content layer or press F6.

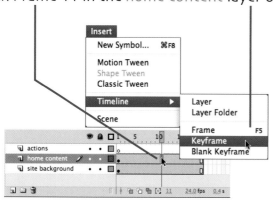

We do this because later we're going to add a text animation that plays when our movie first loads. Keyframe 1 will contain the text animation, and Keyframe 11 will contain static text, while the contents of the site background layer remain the same.

add frame labels

Frame labels let you name frames for logical reference.
(See extra bits on page 51.)

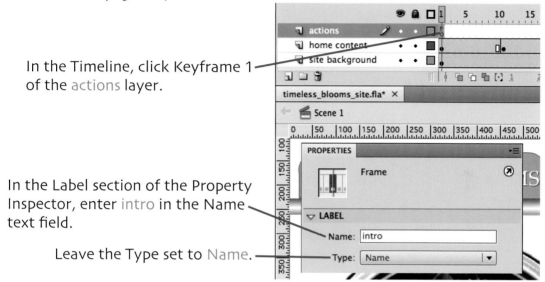

In the Timeline, click Keyframe 1 of the actions layer.

In the Label section of the Property Inspector, enter intro in the Name text field.

Leave the Type set to Name.

Note that Keyframe 1 in the Timeline now displays a flag signifying that it has a label. Also, because this keyframe has a span of several more frames, Flash has room to display the frame label in the Timeline.

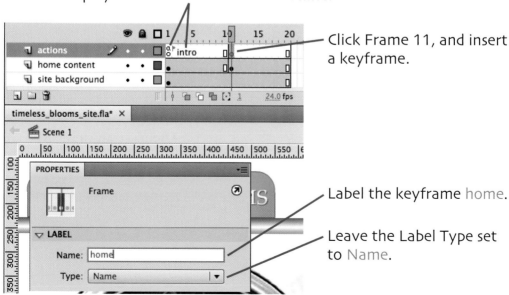

Click Frame 11, and insert a keyframe.

Label the keyframe home.

Leave the Label Type set to Name.

control the timeline

By default, the Playhead in a Flash movie plays through all the frames in a Timeline and loops endlessly unless you tell it otherwise. We use ActionScript to control the Playhead. (See extra bits on Page 52.)

Choose Window > Actions to open the Actions panel. The left side of the panel, the Actions Toolbox, displays a hierarchical list of scripting elements, including classes, methods, functions, and other scripting things we're going to try not to deal with! Just understand that for each list entry there is an associated set of instructions that are executed when it or a subentry are used in a script.

We want to stop the Playhead in Keyframe intro by adding a Stop action.

Click Keyframe intro in the actions layer to select it.

1 Confirm that Action-Script 3.0 is selected in the Actions Filter drop-down menu at the top of the Actions Toolbox.

2 Scroll the Actions Toolbox down until you see the flash.display class entry. This category includes most of the ActionScript classes for controlling playback.

3 Click flash.display to expand the list.

4 Scroll the toolbox down, and then locate and select MovieClip.

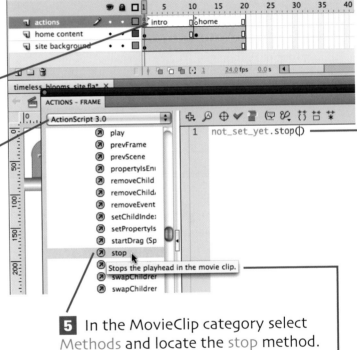

5 In the MovieClip category select Methods and locate the stop method.

6 Note that when you move your mouse over the stop entry, a tooltip gives a brief description of what it is used for.

7 Double-click stop.

A line of code is added in the Script pane.

The line of code consists of two parts, separated by a dot (.).

Remember that in our Flash movie we've already defined several different movie clips and will create many more as our project progresses. Each of them includes its own Timeline. When we use a command like stop, we have to tell Flash which Timeline we're trying to control by providing a path to that Timeline. (It's not always the Timeline in which the ActionScript is included.)

We don't know the path so we'll use a handy feature to help us.

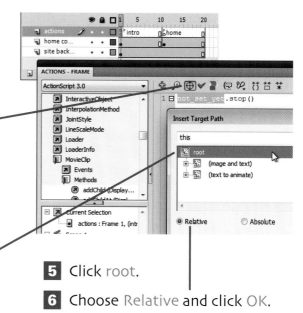

1 Double-click the text not_set_yet to select the code.

2 In the Toolbar, click the Insert a Target Path button.

3 The Insert Target Path dialog shows us the hierarchy, or path, of all the objects currently placed in our movie that are controllable with the stop command.

4 We are controlling the main Timeline of our .fla file, the highest-level Timeline referred to in Action-Script as the root.

5 Click root.

6 Choose Relative and click OK.

The Insert Target Path feature interprets the path we specified to the correct code this, telling Flash the stop command is controlling THIS Timeline—the one in which the code resides.

control the timeline (cont.)

In the Timeline, note that an a is displayed in the keyframe intro, signifying that this frame has ActionScript in it.

Now click the home keyframe, and repeat the steps to add a Stop action to it.

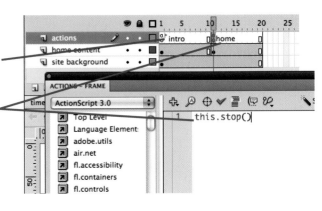

Congratulations! You've just added ActionScript to control your movie!

Let's take a moment to put the Actions panel into the Panels Dock since we'll be using it extensively throughout the rest of the book.

Click the Title Bar, the area above and beside the Actions tab, and drag it over the Panels Dock.

Position the pointer between two panel groups in the Dock. A blue line will appear indicating a Drop Zone where the panel will be placed.

Release the panel.

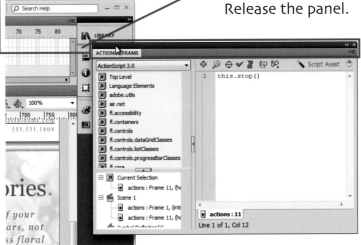

extra bits

frames & keyframes p. 45

- Every Flash movie contains multiple Timelines. Every scene has a main Timeline, and each symbol has its own independent Timeline, as you saw when editing the gr_siteFramework symbol.

  Within a scene or symbol, each layer also has its own Timeline. In complex Flash movies like the one we're building, it is best to use the scene's main Timeline for organizational and reference purposes only. Use the Timelines available inside symbols for animation.

- In the Timeline, keyframes are marked with a bullet. A solid bullet signifies that the keyframe has contents, and a hollow bullet signifies an empty keyframe. The final frame in a keyframe span is marked with a hollow rectangle.

- We define two kinds of frames in a Timeline—basic frames and keyframes. Keyframes are where we do all of our work. Whenever you want to manually change the contents of a frame, you must do it in a keyframe. Basic frames make up what is known as a keyframe's span—the frames between that keyframe and the next. Frames act merely as clones of the preceding keyframe.

- By default, the first frame in any Timeline is a keyframe.

- If you change an object in a frame, you're actually making that change to the keyframe and all frames in its span. It can be incredibly painful to make a change in a particular frame, thinking that you're only changing that frame, and 30 minutes later realize you actually changed 15 frames, so be careful that you are always editing in a keyframe.

add frame labels p. 47

- When you're working with multiple Timelines throughout your movie, moving objects from place to place, and adding or removing frames as you work, it can be difficult to remember what frame number holds an object you're looking for or want to link to from elsewhere in the movie.

  If you have objects on a keyframe at Frame 70 but then add 8 frames to the Timeline, your keyframe is now at 78. If buttons or other movie clips are linking to that keyframe by number, you have to remember to search them out and change the link from 70 to 78. But if you've labeled the keyframe important_frame, that doesn't change, and all the pointers in your movie that point to important_frame are still correct.

continues on next page

extra bits (cont.)

- It's a common practice in Flash development to add frames after a keyframe just to make enough room to display the frame label, making it easy to locate frames during development. In our Timeline so far, the only frames that will actually be seen by viewers are Frames 1 and 11; the other frames will be bypassed. You'll understand this more when we add animations and navigation controlled with ActionScript later in the book.

control the timeline p. 48

- To help keep us organized, we add an empty layer named actions to each of our Timelines—using the layer only for labeling and Action-Script. This helps us keep the mechanics of our movie separate from the content and lets us visually track frame properties easily.

- ActionScript is Flash's powerful scripting language that allows developers to control playback and establish complex interactions. While it is considered an easy language to use, those of us who are not programmers don't necessarily think so.

  Flash does provide some features, like Script Assist mode, that help novices develop scripts, but even using Script Assist effectively requires some understanding of what's going on.

  Throughout the book we'll both create some ActionScript on our own to learn some basics and use the Script Assist feature to get us over some of the hurdles.

  Truly being able to create complex ActionScript interactions requires knowledge of the principles of object-oriented programming—a topic that is well beyond the scope of this book.

6. add animation to your web site

By now you might be thinking "Enough with the boring stuff. I want to make things fly across the Stage." If that's the case, then you're going to love this chapter. Here we add the pizzazz to our Web site that separates it from an ordinary HTML-based site. In the following pages we'll do these tasks:

Use Motion Presets to quickly apply a typical animation.

Tween a Filter Effect to enhance an animation.

Use the 3D Rotation tool to rotate text in 3D space.

Create and save custom Motion Tweens.

Edit animation properties using the Motion Editor.

Use ActionScript to pause playback and play animations at just the right moment.

use motion presets

The first piece of the animated intro we'll create in this chapter will slide part of our text into place from off Stage. To create the animation, we apply a prepackaged animation to the text, setting up the beginning and ending states, and let Flash interpolate, or tween, the in-between frames. (See extra bits on page 72.)

In the Timeline, move the Playhead to Keyframe intro and select the symbol instance text to animate that contains the text "capture memories.".

Double-click the instance to invoke symbol-editing mode.

Click away to deselect all and then [Shift]-click to select the capture and . (period) text containers.

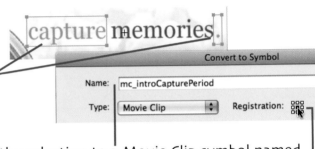

Convert the selection to a Movie Clip symbol named mc_introCapturePeriod, with center registration.

With the new instance still selected, [Shift]-click memories. Right-click (Windows) or [Control]-click (Mac), and choose Distribute to Layers from the drop-down menu.

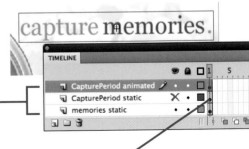

In the Timeline, two new layers are created. The original layer remains but is empty; change its name to CapturePeriod animated. Rename the middle layer CapturePeriod static and the bottom layer memories static.

Click Frame 1 in layer CapturePeriod static and choose Edit > Copy. Make the layer Capture-Period static invisible.

6 add animation to your web site

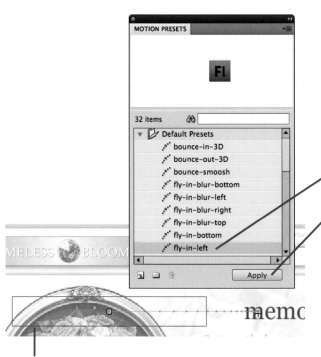

Click Frame 1 in layer Capture-Period animated and choose Edit > Paste in Place.

Choose Window > Motion Presets to open the Motion Presets panel.

In the panel's Default Presets folder, click fly-in-left and note the example preview. (Shift)-click Apply. Pressing (Shift) indicates the target object, the selected instance, is in its ending state.

A 24-frame tween is created, with Frame 1 containing the instance offset to the left with an Alpha value of 0 making it transparent.

Click the right edge of the bounding box, press and hold (Shift), and drag the instance completely off the Stage to the left.

Click away to deselect the instance.

That's it. You just created your first tweened animation.

You can preview an animation inside the Flash application. Let's watch the animation we just created. Move the Playhead to Frame 1 and choose Control > Play, or press (←Enter).

tween properties

To further enhance the animation, let's blur the text as it slides in to give the appearance of a motion trail. We'll add a Blur filter and have Flash tween it. We'll also change the beginning alpha value to make the text visible sooner.

Move the Playhead back to Frame 1.

Click to select the instance. This can be difficult since the symbol is transparent, but click where you think the text should be. If necessary, switch the layer to outlines and you'll be able to see the text.

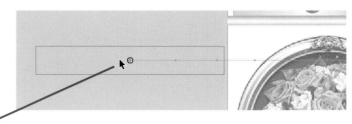

In the Color Effect section of the Property Inspector, change the Alpha value to 35.

In the Filters section, click the Add Filter button and choose Blur from the drop-down menu.

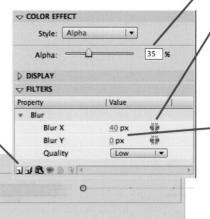

Click the Lock icon to unlink the X and Y values.

Set the Blur X value to 40 and the Blur Y value to 0 to blur only left and right.

Move the Playhead to Frame 24 and select the instance.

In the Filters section, set both Blur values to 0.

Press ⏎Enter to view the animation now.

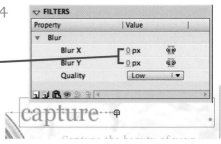

create shape tween

Next we'll create a Shape tween to create an animation in which text zooms in, seemingly from behind the viewer. (See extra bits on page 73.)

Click Keyframe 1 in layer memories static and copy the text to the clipboard.

Insert a new layer named moments zoom above layer CapturePeriod animated and choose Edit > Paste in Place.

With the Text tool, change the text to moments.

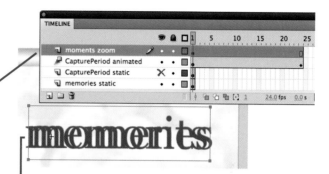

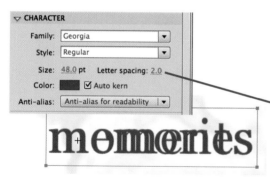

Choose the Selection tool, and select the moments text box.

moments is not as wide as memories, meaning the word spaces will be too big. In the Property Inspector, adjust Letter Spacing to 2 to make it wider.

Copy moments to the clipboard, insert a new layer named moments rotate, and choose Edit > Paste in Place.

Make memories static and moments rotate invisible.

In the layer moments zoom, insert a Keyframe in Frame 24.

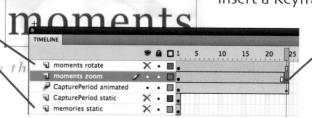

Select moments, choose Modify > Break Apart and then choose Modify > Break Apart again. This converts the text to shapes.

6 add animation to your web site   **57**

create shape tween (cont.)

Move the Playhead to Frame 1 and select moments.

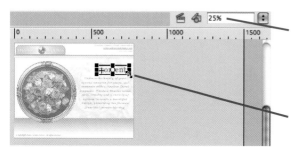

For the next step we need to see as much of the Pasteboard as possible. In the Edit Bar, click the Magnification drop-down and choose 25%.

Select the Free Transform tool. Move the pointer over the bottom-right transformation handle until the cursor changes to the diagonal arrows cursor.

Shift-click and drag down and to the right into the Pasteboard until the letters are taller than the Stage.

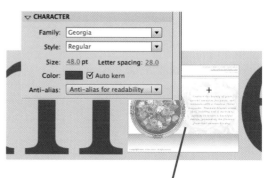

Choose the Selection tool.

Adjust Letter Spacing to 28. Click the text on the stage and use the arrow keys to nudge the text until the Stage is visible between the m and the e.

Choose Modify > Break Apart twice. Click away to deselect.

In the Timeline, right-click (Windows) or Control-click (Mac) Keyframe 1 in the moments zoom layer and choose Create Shape Tween from the drop-down menu.

Return to 100% magnification. From this point in the book I won't instruct you to change your magnification. You should adjust magnification to what works best for you.

Press ←Enter to view the animation now.

use the 3d rotation tool

Next we'll use 3D transformations and tweens to create an animation where moments rotates out and memories rotates in. (See extra bits on page 73.)

Make the moments zoom layer invisible and moments rotate visible.

Select moments and convert it to a Movie Clip symbol named mc_momentsRotate with center registration.

Right-click (Windows) or Control-click (Mac) Frame 1 of layer moments rotate and choose Create Motion Tween from the drop-down menu.

Click Frame 24 of the layer.

Select the 3D Rotation tool and click to turn Global Transform off in the Options section of the Tools panel.

In the 3D Position and View section of the Property Inspector, change the Perspective Angle to 90.

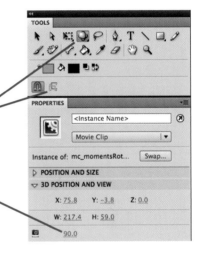

A 3D rotation control is displayed on top of the text. Move the pointer over the green line on the right side of the 3D rotation control. The cursor changes to indicate that this line controls the Y axis.

Click and drag the line down, rotating the text in 3D space. Release when the text becomes completely invisible as if you're viewing it from the side.

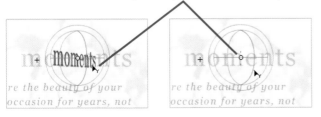

Press ⏎Enter to view the new animation.

modify motion tweens

With the basic rotation animation established, we'll make adjustments to two attributes. First we'll scale the text as it rotates to give it more of an appearance of coming toward the viewer and we'll set easing. Easing is the gradual acceleration or deceleration during an animation that gives animations a realistic appearance.

With the Selection tool, click Frame 12 in the moments rotate layer.

In the Panels Dock, click the Transform icon to open the Transform panel.

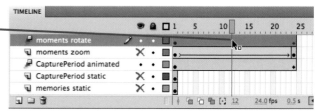

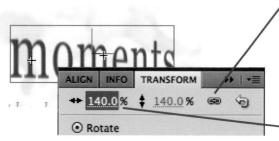

In the Scale section, if the Constrain icon displays a broken chain, click the button to relink the Scale Width and Scale Height values.

Change the Scale Width value to 140.

Press ⏎Enter, the animation will play to the end of the tween.

Press ⏎Enter again to view the complete animation.

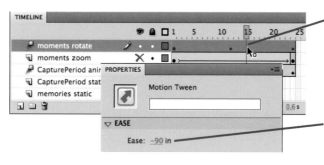

In the Timeline, click a frame in the moments rotate tween span to select the tween.

In the Ease section of the Property Inspector, set the Ease value to -90 to ease into the tween—starting slow and then gaining speed.

Preview the animation again.

save motion presets

We can save custom Motion Tweens to apply to other objects in this or any other Flash file. We'll apply our Motion Tween to memories to establish the foundation of the animation we want for it.

Right-click (Windows) or [Control]-click (Mac) in the moments rotate tween span and choose Save as Motion Preset in the drop-down menu.

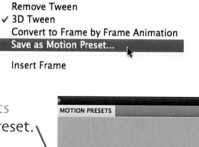

In the Save Preset As dialog, name the preset 3D Rotate Out and click OK.

In the Custom Presets folder in the Motion Presets dialog, note the addition of the 3D Rotate Out preset.

Move the Playhead to Frame 1.

Make layer moments rotate invisible and memories static visible.

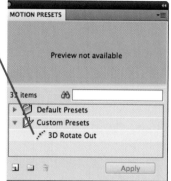

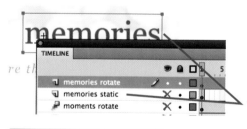

Drag layer memories static to the top of the list and copy memories to the clipboard. Insert a new layer named memories rotate and choose Edit > Paste in Place.

Make layer memories static invisible.

In layer memories rotate, convert memories to a Movie Clip symbol named mc_memoriesRotate with center registration.

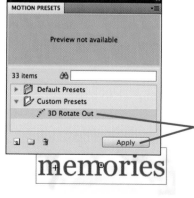

With the instance selected, click 3D Rotate Out in the Motion Presets dialog and click Apply.

Close the Motion Presets dialog. Press [←Enter] to view the animation.

That's a good start. Next we'll make adjustments to the animation properties.

motion editor

We want to change the tween so that it appears to be the completion of the rotation started by the word moments. We'll use the Motion Editor to make changes to properties within the tween to achieve that.

The Motion Editor includes a list of properties that can be tweened, along with numeric values for those properties as well as graphic representations of the curves of each property's tween across the span of the tween. We can adjust properties by editing values in the Value column or by directly manipulating the curves in the Graph column.

First, we want the text to rotate in, not out. In the Timeline, right-click (Windows) or [Control]-click (Mac) in the memories rotate tween span and choose Reverse Keyframes in the drop-down menu.

Choose Window > Motion Editor. The Motion Editor will appear grouped with the Timeline.

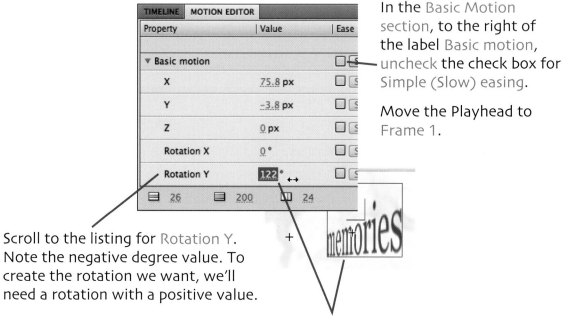

In the Basic Motion section, to the right of the label Basic motion, uncheck the check box for Simple (Slow) easing.

Move the Playhead to Frame 1.

Scroll to the listing for Rotation Y. Note the negative degree value. To create the rotation we want, we'll need a rotation with a positive value.

Click the value and drag to the right. As you drag you'll see the object on Stage, rotating back from its "on edge" position to its original "head-on" position, and then rotate away on the left side.

Release the mouse when the text is once again invisible or "on edge."

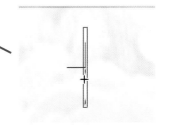

Drag the Playhead (this is called scrubbing) from Frame 1 to Frame 24. Note the change in the 3D rotation.

Click the check box next to the Basic Motion label to turn easing back on.

Scroll to the Transformation section. Uncheck the easing check box next to the label Transformation.

Scroll to the listings for Scale X and Scale Y.

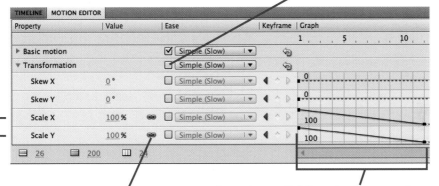

Note that the solid line indicates the tween from 140% scale to 100% occurs between Frames 1 and 12. To make this rotation mirror the moments rotation, we need the tween to occur between Frames 12 and 24.

Click the Link icon to unlink the Scale X and Scale Y values.

motion editor (cont.)

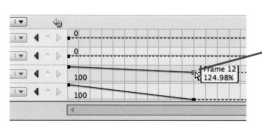

To change the Scale X tween:

1 Click the square Keyframe handle in Frame 12 and drag up.

Note the tool tip showing feedback on the percentage as you drag. Release the handle at 140%.

2 Move the Playhead to Frame 24. In the Keyframe column, click the Add Keyframe control.

Note the addition of a Keyframe handle in Frame 24.

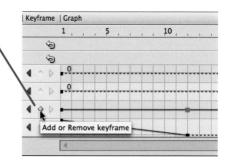

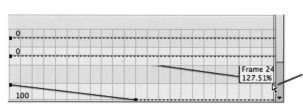

3 Click the Keyframe handle in Frame 24 and drag down. Release the handle at 100%.

You can adjust the value in the Value column if you have difficulty getting exactly 100%.

Repeat steps 1–3 to change the Scale Y tween.

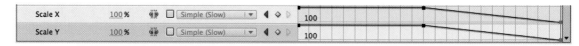

Click the check box to turn easing back on.

In the Eases section, change the Simple (Slow) value to positive 90.

Press ⏎Enter to view the animation.

rearrange frames

Switch back to the Timeline panel and turn visibility on for all the layers. Press (←Enter) to view the animations we've created. Kind of a mess with them all playing at the same time!

Now it's time to work on timing the animations to occur at different times by moving frames and tween spans around in the Timeline.

In the Timeline, right-click (Windows) or (Control)-click (Mac) any frame and choose Select All Frames from the drop-down menu.

Right-click (Windows) or (Control)-click (Mac) on the selected frames and choose Cut Frames from the drop-down menu.

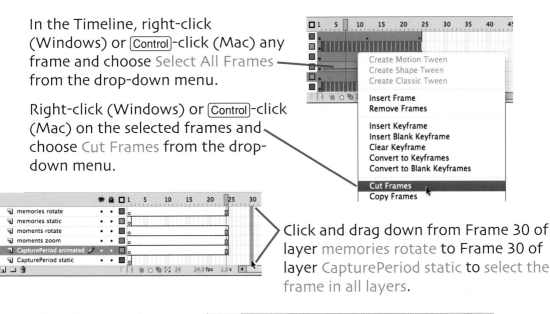

Click and drag down from Frame 30 of layer memories rotate to Frame 30 of layer CapturePeriod static to select the frame in all layers.

Right-click (Windows) or (Control)-click (Mac) on the selected frames and choose Paste Frames from the drop-down.

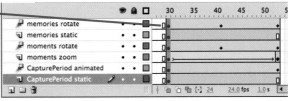

The first animation to begin playing will be the animation on the CapturePeriod animated layer. When that animation completes, we need the static version of the text to display while the other animations play, so we need to move the first populated frame of layer CapturePeriod static to Frame 54—the first frame after the animation completes.

rearrange frames (cont.)

Click anywhere in the Timeline to deselect all frames.

Click Frame 30 in layer CapturePeriod static, then (Shift)-click Frame 53.

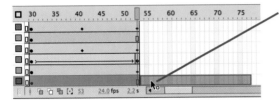

Click in the selection and drag to the right. Use the blue feedback to release the frames when the first frame of the selection is over Frame 54.

Next we'll change the moments zoom animation to start a few frames after the CapturePeriod animation starts.

You can move a Keyframe by selecting it and then dragging it.

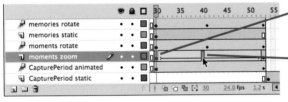

Click Keyframe 30 in the moments zoom layer to select it.

Click again and drag the Keyframe to the right, moving it to Frame 40.

Now click Keyframe 53. Click and drag it to Frame 70. This will also increase the length of the animation from 24 frames (2 seconds) to 30 frames (2.5).

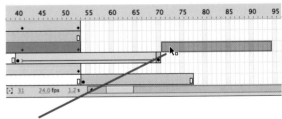

The entire span of a motion tween can be selected by clicking anywhere within the span. Click in the moments rotate motion tween span to select it.

Click and drag the span to the right until the first frame is at Frame 71—the first frame after the moments zoom animation ends.

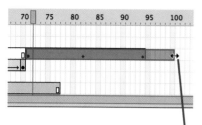

To increase the length of this animation slightly, move your cursor over the right edge of Property Keyframe 94. The cursor changes to a left-right arrow.

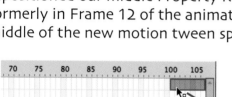

Click and drag over Frame 100 and release. Note that Flash re-interpolated our tween and repositioned our middle Property Keyframe, formerly in Frame 12 of the animation, to the middle of the new motion tween span.

Now click to select the memories rotate motion tween span. Click and drag it until the first frame is at Frame 101—the first frame after the moments rotate tween ends.

Again, increase the length to 30 frames by moving the last Property Keyframe to Frame 130.

Finally, insert a Keyframe in Frame 131 in layer memories static.

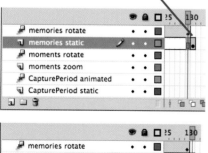

Click Frame 130 of layer memories static and delete the text that is on the Stage.

Press ⏎Enter to view the animations.

It looks great except capture and the period disappear about halfway through.

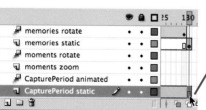

Click Frame 131 in the CapturePeriod static layer. Choose Insert > Timeline > Frame.

Press ⏎Enter to view the animations now.

pause an animation

The animation looks great, but it all flies by too fast. We want to add a pause after moments zooms in and before it rotates, holding the word in place long enough for it to register with the viewer. (See extra bits on page 73.)

In the Timeline, add a new layer named actions at the top of the Layers column.

In the actions layer, select Frame 70 and add a keyframe.

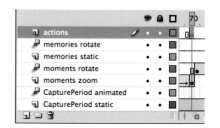

Open the Actions panel.

Enter the code as shown code in the Script pane: The code needs to be typed exactly as shown and it is case-sensitive.

This code stops the Timeline.

This line creates a Timer object.

This sets the duration of the timer to 2000 milliseconds (2 seconds).

This says to wait for the duration only one time.

This tells Flash what to do when the timer completes, which is to execute the function timerHandler.

This starts the timer.

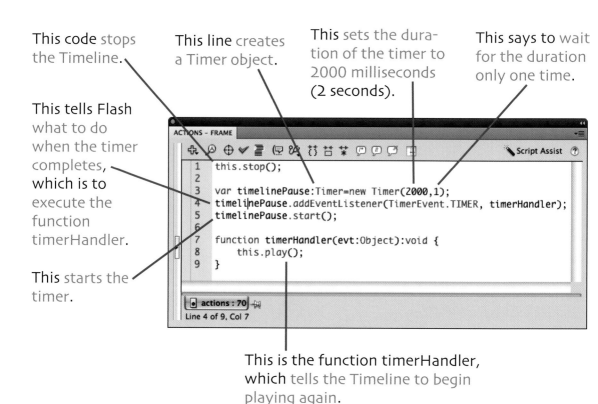

```
1   this.stop();
2
3   var timelinePause:Timer=new Timer(2000,1);
4   timelinePause.addEventListener(TimerEvent.TIMER, timerHandler);
5   timelinePause.start();
6
7   function timerHandler(evt:Object):void {
8       this.play();
9   }
```

This is the function timerHandler, which tells the Timeline to begin playing again.

preview your movie

Up to this point, we've previewed our animations in the Flash workspace. To preview the effect of the ActionScript pause, however, the animation has to be exported as a SWF file and viewed in the Flash Player.

We can do that quickly without going through the publishing process.

Choose Control > Test Movie, or press Ctrl ←Enter (Windows) or ⌘ ←Enter (Mac).

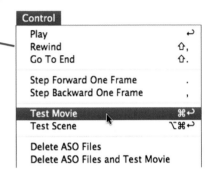

Flash quickly exports the SWF, opens a new Flash Player window, and plays the animation.

Notice the pause on the word moments; our ActionScript is working.

The animation loops because we haven't set any ActionScript in the final frame of the Timeline to stop it. We'll fix that later.

Click the Close button to close the Flash Player window.

control movie clips

We need to stop the animation from repeating, and we also need to move our main Flash movie past the intro animation to the home frame. We'll do that with more ActionScript.

In the actions layer, select Frame 131 and insert a Keyframe.

In the Script Pane enter a Stop command, this.stop();.

Remember that our text to animate movie clip is playing in Keyframe intro of our main Timeline. Once the animations are complete, we want to move the main Timeline forward to Keyframe home, which will be visually identical but without the animation. Home is the Keyframe that users will navigate to and from as they move around the site. We do this so that users only see the animation when they first enter the site.

With Keyframe 131 still selected, enter this code in the Script Pane:

MovieClip(this.root).gotoAndStop("home");

This code tells Flash to move the movie's root Timeline to Keyframe home and stop.

That's it. Our intro animation is complete. We only need to do one more step to make everything work the way we want.

In the Edit Bar select Scene 1 to return to our main Timeline. Select Keyframe home in the actions layer. Because the text to animate symbol has no content in the first frame, the text Capture Memories. is not visible. Leaving the movie clip here as is would result in the text animation playing again when the Playhead moves to home.

Symbol types (Movie Clip, Button, Image) can be redefined on instances without changing the symbol's internal type. We'll do this to display the text we want.

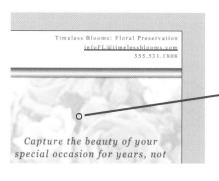

Because text to animate has no visible contents, its presence on the Stage is indicated by and can be selected via the Registration Point marker.

Make sure you're on the selection tool, and then click the Registration Point marker.

In the Property Inspector, click the Instance Behavior drop-down and choose Graphic.

In the Looping section of the Property Inspector, click the Options drop-down and choose Single Frame. Enter 131 (the final frame of the text to animate symbol) in the First Frame text field.

The text appears just as we want.

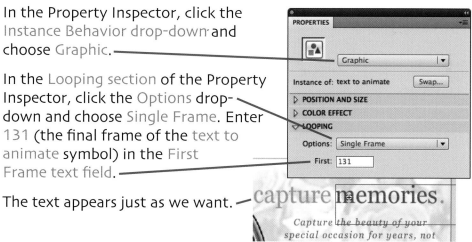

Press Ctrl ←Enter (Windows) or ⌘ ←Enter (Mac) to preview your work in the Flash Player window.

extra bits

use motion presets p. 54

- An animation is a series of static images (frames), where objects change incrementally from a beginning point to an end point. In Flash, we can define the beginning and end states and let Flash generate the incremental frames. This method of creating the in-between frames is called tweening.

- There are four types of tweens in Flash: motion, shape, classic, and inverse kinematic. We will only use motion and shape. Motion tween is a bit of a misnomer, as it can be used to create changes not only in placement (motion) but also in alpha transparency, size, rotation, skew, and color effect. Motion tweens are applied to keyframes in a layer and only work when the layer contains only one symbol instances or text block.

  Shape tweens work on shapes, not symbols or text blocks, and are used to change or "morph" the appearance of the shape.

- Different types of tweens and there states are represented in the Timeline with different indicators. A span of frames with a blue background indicates a motion tween. A black dot in the first frame indicates the presence of a valid target object and black diamonds indicate Property keyframes that contain property changes.
  A span of frames with a light green background indicates a shape tween. A solid black arrow indicates the presence of valid tween objects on both keyframes. A dashed line indicates a broken tween.

- Ah, the Flash intro to a Web site—probably the most reviled Web phenomenon since the HTML Blink tag. The interminable wait to see the content you came to the site for in the first place and the frantic search for a Skip button, hoping the developer included one, made it all too much to bear and sent many viewers fleeing without ever getting into the site.

  So what will we do? Create an intro, of course! However, we're going to create one that's done the right way—the evolved way. Here are the rules we'll follow to ensure that the animation doesn't irritate our viewers and doesn't get in the way of our content, which is, after all, the reason for having the site. The guidelines and how we're following them are as follows:

  Make it simple and meaningful. Our animation will be elegant while actually furthering Timeless

Blooms' marketing message of capturing the emotion of special events.

Don't let your intro obscure real content and navigation. Allow users to "get on with it" without waiting for the intro to finish. Our content and navigation buttons will be available from Frame 1.

Once viewers have seen the animation, don't make them view it again when navigating back to the home page from other areas of the site. This is why we created two keyframes in our main Timeline, one for the intro and one for home.

create shape tween p. 57

New layers added to the Timeline automatically match the number of frames used elsewhere in the Timeline.

use the 3D rotation tool p. 59

- When an object with a 3D transformation is placed in a movie clip symbol, that symbol can no longer be edited in place. After using the 3D Rotation tool, if you exit symbol-editing mode during this chapter to come back to it later you will not see the site framework or the framed bouquet image and text when you re-enter symbol-editing mode on the text to animate symbols.

- The initial release of Flash CS4 Professional included an apparent bug in which 3D rotations changed their appearance in the Flash application when reopened after initially being set up. However, the rotation appeared correctly in movies published after that time. This may have been fixed in subsequent updates.

pause an animation p. 68

- We could add frames between the animation segments here, but our 2-second pause would require adding 24 blank frames. Our Timeline is already long and unwieldy. Instead, we'll use ActionScript to pause the Timeline.

- As a beginning Flash developer without deep understanding of ActionScript or other programming languages, you can often find code examples to use without understanding the technicalities of what they do.

There are many resources on the Web that provide such examples. Visit the Adobe Developer Forums at www.adobe.com/support/forums/. continues on next page

extra bits

Also, you can type a question like "how to pause a movie in Flash" in a Web search engine like Google and get pointers to multiple developer sites offering code help.

- The code we use in this step is very simple. You can copy and paste it into any of your projects to create a pause in animation.

7. build a navigation system

So far, we've created a great-looking home page with an engaging introductory animation. But the site doesn't have any real content yet. It's like a movie with opening credits but no scenes revealing the plot.

In this chapter, we add keyframes to the main Timeline to define the site's sections, and create interactive buttons to navigate between those sections.

add sections to the site

Before we create buttons for navigating the site, we need to have some places to navigate to. We need to add the other sections of our site to the Timeline.

The Web site has four sections: Home, Info, Gallery, and Pricing.

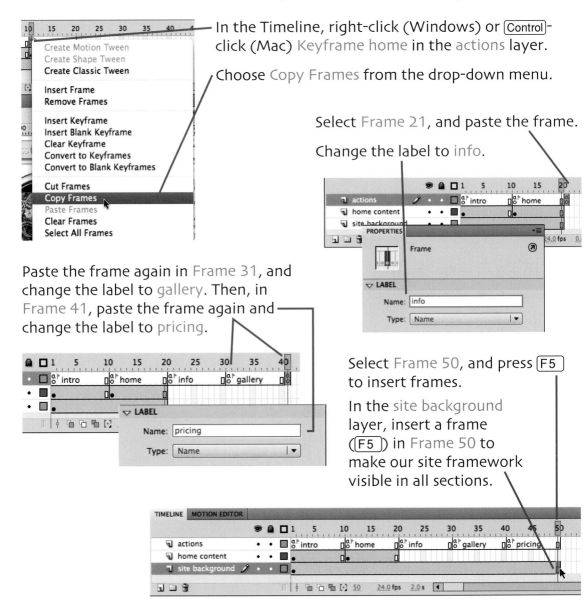

In the Timeline, right-click (Windows) or Control-click (Mac) Keyframe home in the actions layer.

Choose Copy Frames from the drop-down menu.

Select Frame 21, and paste the frame.

Change the label to info.

Paste the frame again in Frame 31, and change the label to gallery. Then, in Frame 41, paste the frame again and change the label to pricing.

Select Frame 50, and press F5 to insert frames.

In the site background layer, insert a frame (F5) in Frame 50 to make our site framework visible in all sections.

Add three new layers, one for each of the sections we've just created. Name them info content, gallery content, and pricing content.

In the info content layer, insert a keyframe in Frame 21.

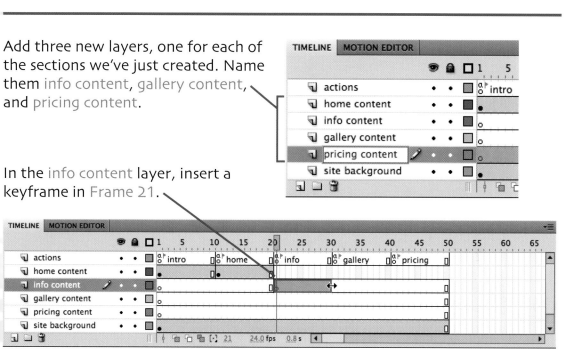

Move the cursor over the right edge of Frame 50. Press and hold Ctrl (Windows) or ⌘ (Mac); the cursor changes to a left-right arrow.

Click and drag to the left. Release on Frame 30. This makes the keyframe span 10 frames from Frame 21 to Frame 30.

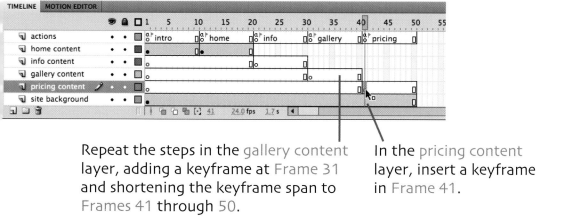

Repeat the steps in the gallery content layer, adding a keyframe at Frame 31 and shortening the keyframe span to Frames 41 through 50.

In the pricing content layer, insert a keyframe in Frame 41.

create buttons

With our sections defined, we need to create a button for each of the sections. Button symbols provide an easy method for creating the type of interactive, multistate button we're accustomed to seeing on the Web. The first step will be to create a button master that will serve as an easily edited template for all of the buttons. (See extra bits on page 94.)

The background appearance of the buttons will be a variation of the linear gradient we used in the site framework. We'll use a copy of the rectangle as a starting point for the button background.

In the Library panel, open the framework parts folder. Double-click the symbol icon for the symbol gr_site-Framework to invoke symbol-editing mode.

Select the rectangle with the linear gradient fill near the top of the Stage.

Copy the rectangle to the clipboard.

Click off the Stage to deselect the rectangle.

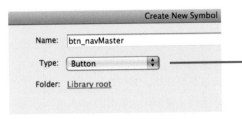

Choose Insert > New Symbol to create a new empty symbol.

In the Create New Symbol dialog, enter btn_navMaster, and choose Button for the Type. Click OK.

Flash creates the new symbol and opens it for editing. Note the special button Timeline with a specially labeled frame for each button state.

Rename Layer 1 button background.

Click the Stage and paste the rectangle.

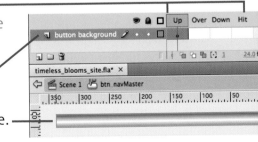

7 build a navigation system

1 In the Position and Size section of the Property Inspector, confirm that the width and height values are not linked. Change the width to 60.

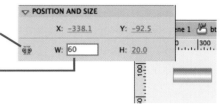

Centering the button parts on the registration point of the button symbol will help make arranging objects easier. We'll center the rectangle now.

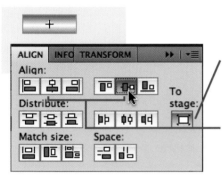

2 With the rectangle still selected, open the Align panel.

3 Click the Align To Stage button to align the rectangle to the symbol's registration point.

4 Click the Align Horizontal Center button and then the Align Vertical Center button to center the rectangle on the registration point.

We'll be working on the button appearance for a while, so it's a good idea to expand our panels. In the Panels Dock, click the double-arrow Expand Panels control in the Panel title bar.

The appearance of the button background in the Over state will be different than that in the Up state. It will still be a variation on the gradient, so let's get the rectangle placed in the Over state before we begin changing it.

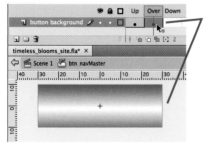

5 In the Timeline, click the Over frame and insert a keyframe, which places a copy of the rectangle in the frame.

create buttons (cont.)

Click back in the Up keyframe, automatically selecting the rectangle.

In the Color panel, double-click the pointer on the left end of the gradient definition bar to open the swatches pop-up. Choose our light purple color.

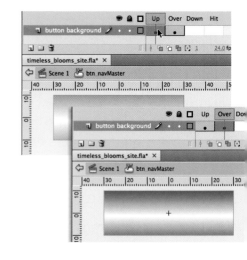

Now we have a different background appearance between the Up and Over states. That's enough for the background for now.

Next we'll add some placeholder text to our button master. Keeping in mind that the text will be changed for each button that is made from this master and knowing that the text will be placed in multiple frames (and even different Timelines later in this chapter), we want to be smart about how we create the text so that changing it will be very easy.

To accomplish this, we'll create a symbol of the text and place instances of that symbol in the places we need it. We'll then be able to change the text only once, but have it update throughout the different frames and Timelines.

Add a new layer and name it button text.

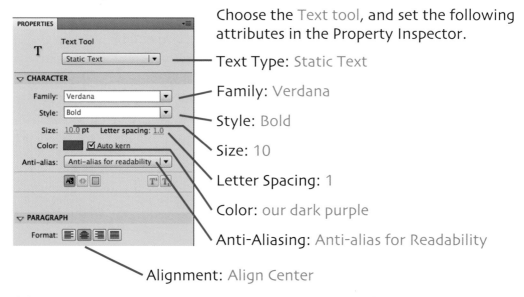

Choose the Text tool, and set the following attributes in the Property Inspector.

Text Type: Static Text

Family: Verdana

Style: Bold

Size: 10

Letter Spacing: 1

Color: our dark purple

Anti-Aliasing: Anti-alias for Readability

Alignment: Align Center

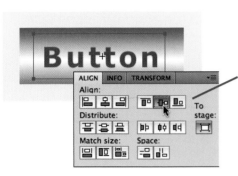

Click the Stage and type Button.

Choose the Selection tool to set the text.

Use the Align panel to center the text box on the registration point.

Convert the text box to a symbol ([F8]).

In the Convert to Symbol dialog enter btn_navMasterText, choose Graphic, and click the center Registration point to help center the text in the button. Click OK.

The Down state is displayed when a user clicks the button. For now we'll define it to be the same as the Over state.

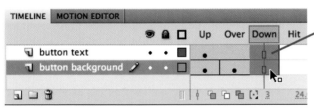

Click the Down frame in the button text layer and drag down to select the frame in the button background layer.

Insert a frame ([F5]).

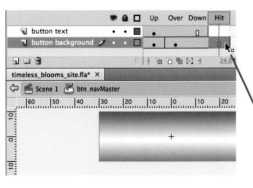

The Hit state defines the area of the button that responds to mouse activity. For our button, that area is the same as the background.

Select frame Hit in the button background layer and insert a frame ([F5]).

We now have the basics of a working button.

preview button actions

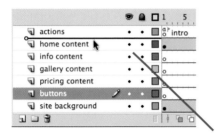

We can preview our button actions inside Flash. Let's place an instance on the Stage and see how our button works so far.

Click Scene 1 in the Edit Bar to exit symbol-editing mode.

Add a new layer to the Timeline, and name it buttons. Position the layer between the home content and actions layers.

In the Library panel, click the btn_navMaster symbol, and drag it onto the Stage over the linear gradient rectangle and near the right edge of the Stage.

Use the Selection tool or arrow keys to position the button instance vertically over the linear gradient rectangle.

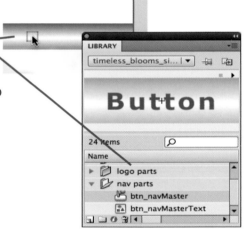

Choose Control > Enable Simple Buttons.

Move the cursor over the button to view the Over state.

Click to view the Down state; right now it's the same as the Over state so you won't see any change.

Our button works great, but it's kind of boring. Let's work on punching it up.

Choose Control > Enable Simple Buttons again to turn off button preview.

animate a button state

To make our button more interesting, we're going to add a short animation to the Over state and add a slight offset to the Down state.

With the Selection tool, double-click the button instance to edit it.

In the Timeline, click the Down frame of the button background layer and insert a keyframe so the animation we create for the Over state won't also be in the Down state.

Click the Over frame of the button background layer, selecting the gradient-filled rectangle.

Convert the selection to a symbol (F8). Name the symbol btn_navMasterOver, choose Movie Clip, and center Registration.

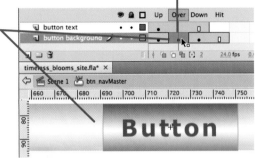

Double-click the new symbol to edit it.

In the Timeline, right-click (Windows) or Control -click (Mac) Frame 1 in Layer 1 and choose Create Shape Tween from the drop-down menu.

Insert a keyframe in Frame 7.

Select the Gradient Transform tool, which is under the Free Transform Tool, and click to select the rectangle.

Click and drag the center point handle down until the top fill guide is below the rectangle. Release the mouse and note where the white area of the gradient is in relation to the white area of the gradient in the rectangle in the background. Continue to adjust the center point handle up or down until the two white areas line up.

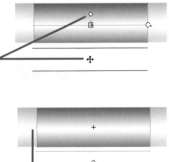

Press (←Enter) to preview the animation.

animate a button (cont.)

We need to add a Stop action, or the animation will loop repeatedly when the user's mouse is over the button.

> Add a new layer and name it actions.

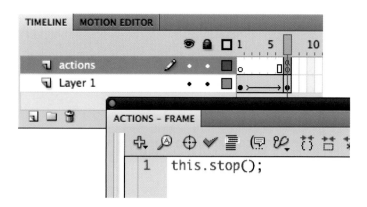

Insert a keyframe in Frame 7.

Enter this.stop(); in the Actions panel.

Now we'll make a small animation of the text.

Click btn_navMaster in the Edit Bar to exit symbol-editing mode for the btn_navMasterOver movie clip.

With the Selection tool, select the Over frame in the button text layer. Insert a keyframe.

Select the Down frame in the button text layer and insert a keyframe.

Click back on the Over frame of the button text layer, automatically selecting the text symbol instance.

Convert the selection to a symbol (F8).

Name the symbol btn_navMasterTextOver, choose Movie Clip for the Type, and choose center Registration.

Use the selection tool to double-click the new symbol to edit it.

In the Timeline, right-click (Windows) or Control-click (Mac) Frame 1 and choose Create Motion Tween from the drop-down menu.

Move the cursor over the right edge of the last frame in the tween span. The cursor will change to the left-right arrow.

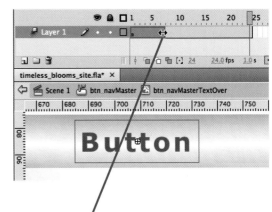

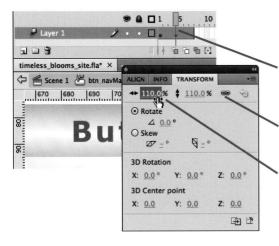

Click and drag to the left. Release the mouse on Frame 7.

Click Frame 4 in the tween span.

Select the instance btn_navMasterText.

In the Transform panel, confirm that the Scale Width and Scale Height are linked.

Change the Scale Width value to 110.

Click Frame 7 in the tween span.

In the Transform panel, set the Scale Width to 100.

Preview the animation.

We need to add a Stop action for this animation.

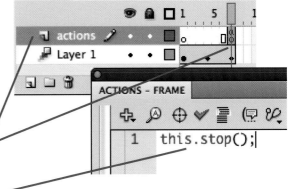

Add a new layer and name it actions.

Insert a keyframe in Frame 7.

Enter this.stop(); in the Actions panel.

7 build a navigation system

animate a button (cont.)

Finally, for our Down state we want to move the text down and to the right one pixel.

Click btn_navMaster in the Edit Bar to exit symbol-editing mode for the movie clip.

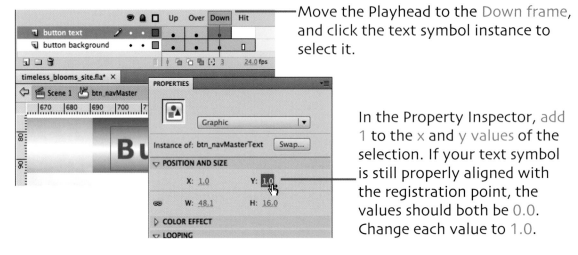

Move the Playhead to the Down frame, and click the text symbol instance to select it.

In the Property Inspector, add 1 to the x and y values of the selection. If your text symbol is still properly aligned with the registration point, the values should both be 0.0. Change each value to 1.0.

We're done editing the button, so exit symbol-editing mode by clicking Scene 1 in the Edit Bar.

The Enable Simple Buttons feature won't show us the animated Over state, so we'll have to preview our buttons in the Flash Player.

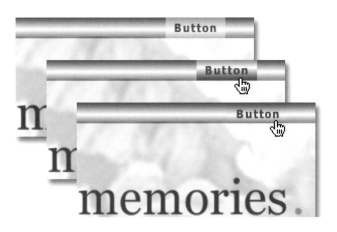

Choose Control > Test Movie, or press Ctrl ↵Enter (Windows) or ⌘ ↵Return (Mac).

Move the cursor over the button to see the Over state animation, then click to see the text offset for the Down state.

Close the Flash Player window.

add button sound

As the final touch to our button, we're going to add a click sound to the Down state.

Choose File > Import > Import to Library. In the Import to Library dialog, navigate to the development_files folder. Select the file btn_click.wav, and click Open.

Double-click the btn_navMaster instance to edit it.

Add a new layer, and name it sound.

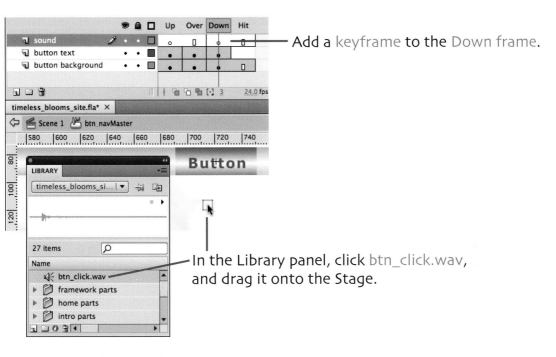

Add a keyframe to the Down frame.

In the Library panel, click btn_click.wav, and drag it onto the Stage.

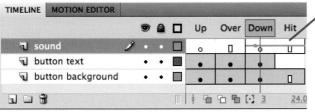

Notice the marker in the Timeline, signifying a sound object in the frame.

Exit symbol-editing mode.

If you want to test the sound, turn on Enable Simple Buttons and click the button.

duplicate buttons

Now that we've completed our button design, we need to make copies for each of the sections of our site.

We'll make duplicates of the different symbols that make up a button and then use symbol swapping to change out one symbol for another. This can be a difficult series of steps, but by using consistent naming conventions for symbols and dividing the steps into three smaller groups, we can do it successfully.

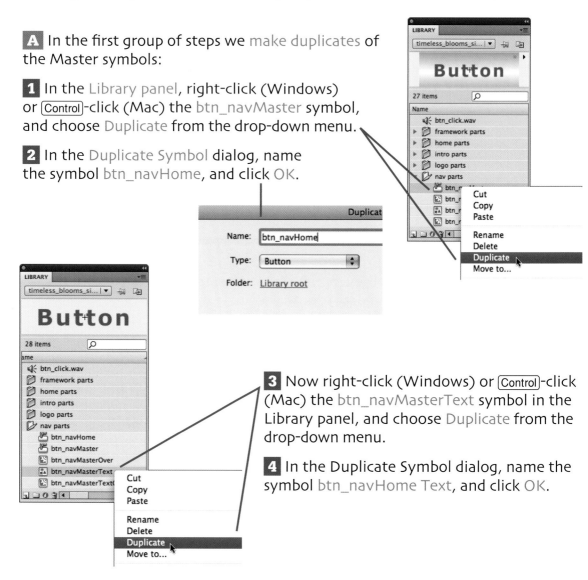

A In the first group of steps we make duplicates of the Master symbols:

1 In the Library panel, right-click (Windows) or Control-click (Mac) the btn_navMaster symbol, and choose Duplicate from the drop-down menu.

2 In the Duplicate Symbol dialog, name the symbol btn_navHome, and click OK.

3 Now right-click (Windows) or Control-click (Mac) the btn_navMasterText symbol in the Library panel, and choose Duplicate from the drop-down menu.

4 In the Duplicate Symbol dialog, name the symbol btn_navHome Text, and click OK.

7 build a navigation system

5 Now right-click (Windows) or [Control]-click (Mac) the btn_navMasterTextOver symbol in the Library panel, and choose Duplicate from the drop-down menu.

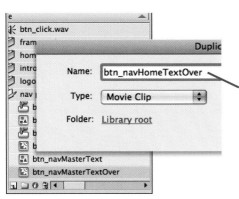

6 In the Duplicate Symbol dialog, name the symbol btn_navHomeTextOver, and click OK.

B Next we change the text in the text symbol to match the section.

In the Library panel, double-click the btn_navHomeText symbol icon to edit it. Change the text to Home.

C In the final series of steps, we'll swap the instances of the Master Symbols with the symbols we've created for that section.

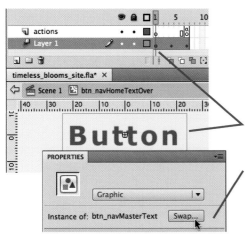

1 In the Library panel, double-click the btn_navHomeTextOver symbol icon to edit it.

2 In Keyframe 1, select the btn_Master-Text symbol instance.

3 Click the Swap Symbol button in the Property Inspector.

duplicate buttons (cont.)

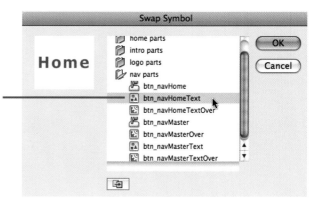

4 In the Swap Symbol dialog, select btn_navHomeText, and click OK.

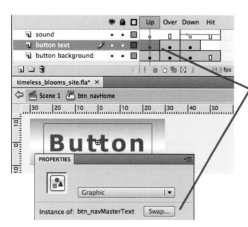

5 Now double-click the btn_navHome symbol icon in the Library panel.

6 Move the Playhead to the Up keyframe and select the btn_navMasterText symbol. In the Property Inspector, click the Swap Symbol button.

7 In the Swap Symbol dialog, select btn_navHomeText, and click OK.

8 Repeat the steps to swap the symbol in the Down keyframe.

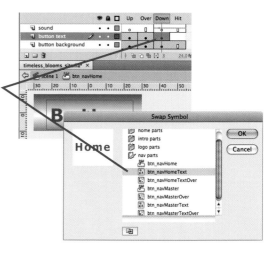

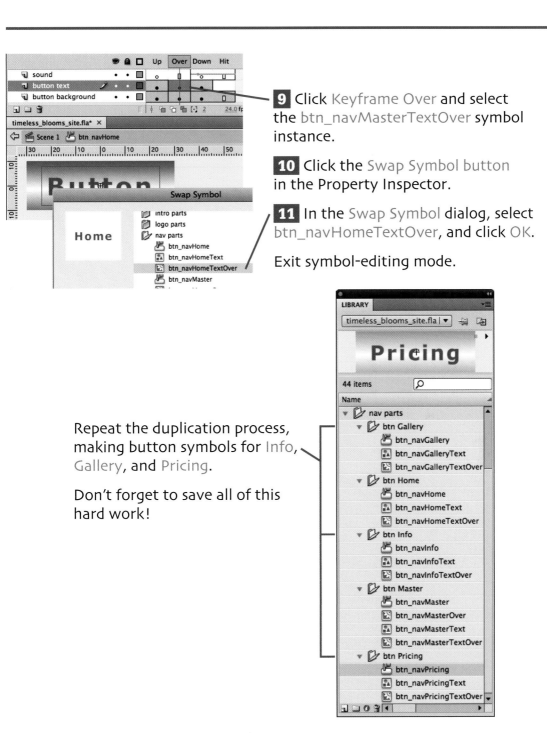

9 Click Keyframe Over and select the btn_navMasterTextOver symbol instance.

10 Click the Swap Symbol button in the Property Inspector.

11 In the Swap Symbol dialog, select btn_navHomeTextOver, and click OK.

Exit symbol-editing mode.

Repeat the duplication process, making button symbols for Info, Gallery, and Pricing.

Don't forget to save all of this hard work!

layout buttons

With a button for each of our sections complete, we can add them to the layout.

In the Edit Bar, confirm that you are not in symbol-editing mode.

First delete the button Master instance from the Stage.

In the layers column of the Timeline, select the buttons layer to make it the current layer.

From the Library panel, drag out an instance of each of the buttons into the buttons layer, ordering them as shown here. (Don't worry about spacing or alignment; we'll fix that in a minute.)

In the layers column of the Timeline, click the buttons layer to select the four button instances on the layer.

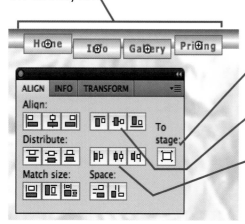

Open the Align panel.

Click the Align to Stage button to turn it off.

Click the Align Vertical Center button to align the buttons.

Click the Distribute Horizontal Center button to evenly space the buttons.

Zoom in to enlarge your view of the buttons.

With the Selection tool, drag to position the buttons accurately on top of the gradient-filled rectangle. If needed, use the arrow keys to nudge them into place.

Click away from the buttons to deselect them. Choose Control > Test Movie, or press Ctrl+⏎Enter (Windows) or ⌘+⏎Return (Mac) to preview the movie in the Flash Player. Test out the buttons to see how they operate.

add actionscript

With our site sections defined and the buttons created to navigate to them, let's hook the two up. We'll use ActionScript to establish functional navigation.

Select the btn_navHome instance. (To select it, you must first deselect all of the buttons.)

In the Property Inspector, enter btnHome for the Instance Name.

Repeat the process for the Info, Gallery, and Pricing buttons as shown.

Select Keyframe intro in the layer actions.

In the Actions panel enter:

btnHome.addEventListener(MouseEvent.CLICK, home);

function home (evt:Event):void {

   gotoAndStop("home");

}

Select the Info button.

In the Actions panel enter the above code again, replacing each of the four occurrences of the word home with info. Note: The Actionscript is case sensitive.

Repeat the process for the Gallery and Pricing buttons.

```
ACTIONS - FRAME
                                                    Script Assist
 1    this.stop();
 2
 3    btnHome.addEventListener(MouseEvent.CLICK, home);
 4    function home(evt:Event):void {
 5        gotoAndStop("home");
 6    }
 7
 8    btnInfo.addEventListener(MouseEvent.CLICK, info);
 9    function info(evt:Event):void {
10        gotoAndStop("info");
11    }
12
13    btnGallery.addEventListener(MouseEvent.CLICK, gallery);
14    function gallery(evt:Event):void {
15        gotoAndStop("gallery");
16    }
17
18    btnPricing.addEventListener(MouseEvent.CLICK, pricing);
19    function pricing(evt:Event):void {
20        gotoAndStop("pricing");
21    }
```

extra bits

create buttons p. 78

- Buttons have different images (referred to as states) that display based upon user action. The Up state displays by default; the Over state displays when the user moves the mouse over the button; and the Down state displays when the button is clicked. A fourth state, Hit, is never displayed but is used to define the active area of the button.

- In most cases, you'll use the same graphic elements for all of your buttons. When you're working out the design, work with the text of the longest name you'll need. This ensures that the graphic fits all of your buttons and you won't have to make frustrating fixes later. In our project, the button was originally sized to the word Gallery button because it is just a bit wider than Pricing.

7 build a navigation system

8. add inside sections of the web site

In this chapter we begin filling in content in the different sections of the site. We'll use both basic and complex techniques to present each different type of content in the most effective way. In this chapter we'll:

Style text with Cascading Style Sheets.

Create input text fields for user interaction.

Load HTML-formatted text on the fly.

Set text dynamically.

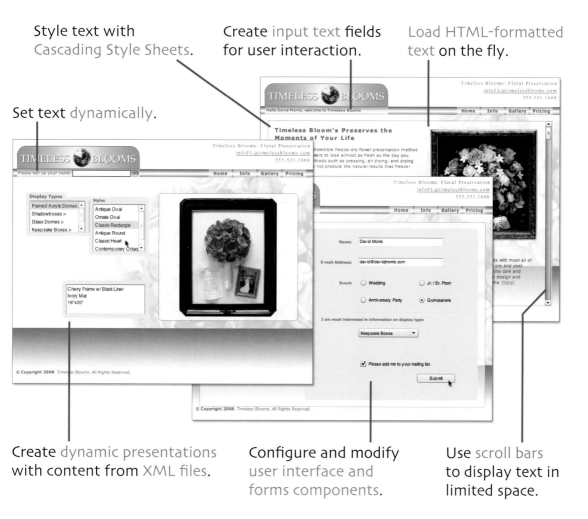

Create dynamic presentations with content from XML files.

Configure and modify user interface and forms components.

Use scroll bars to display text in limited space.

import symbols

The benefits of symbols as reusable and easy-to-update objects are not limited to their use in a single document. You can import symbols from other files and maintain a link to the original source, allowing quick updates to objects in multiple files. On a large site with multiple Flash files or if you have symbols that you use time and again, importing symbols from a single source can be a great time-saver.

You can open a file's library without opening the complete Flash file.

Open the Library panel if it's not already open.

Select File > Import > Open External Library.

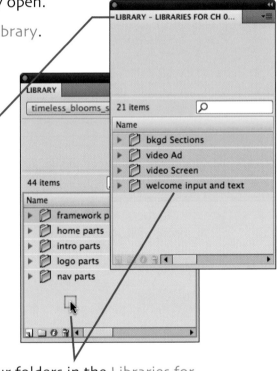

In the Open as Library dialog, navigate to the development_files folder. Select the file Libraries for Ch 08 and Ch 09.fla, and click Open.

A new Library panel with the file's symbols is opened.

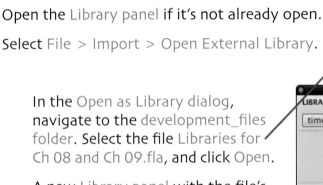

Select the four folders in the Libraries for Chapter 08 and Ch 09.fla library and drag and drop them into the timeless_blooms_site.fla library.

The folders and the symbols they contain are now in timeless_blooms_site.fla.

Close the Library panel for Libraries for Ch 08 and Ch 09.fla.

update symbols

To update a symbol shared between files, we make changes to the symbol in the original source file and then pull the updates into the other files with instances of the symbol.

Let's make an update to one of the symbols we just imported.

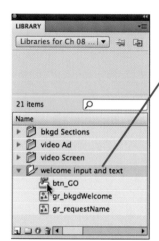

Open the file Libraries for Ch 08 and Ch 09.fla.

In the Library panel, open the folder welcome input and text.

Double-click the symbol icon for btn_GO to invoke symbol-editing mode on the button.

With the Selection tool, click to select the GO text box.

In the Character section of the Property Inspector, click the Text (fill) color well, and choose our dark purple.

Save the file (File > Save) and close it.

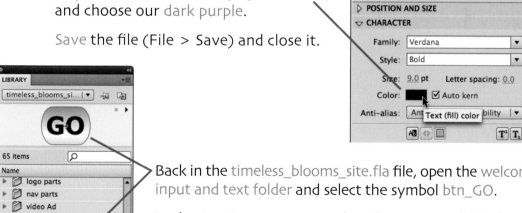

Back in the timeless_blooms_site.fla file, open the welcome input and text folder and select the symbol btn_GO.

In the Preview pane, note that the text is still black.

Right-click (Windows) or Control-click (Mac) the selected symbol and choose Properties from the drop-down menu.

8 add inside sections of the web site   **97**

update symbols (cont.)

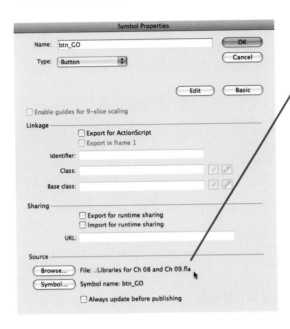

In the Symbol Properties dialog, click Advanced to expand the dialog.

In the Source area, note that Libraries for Ch 08 and Ch 09.fla is shown as the source.

Click OK to close the dialog.

Right-click (Windows) or Control-click (Mac) the symbol btn_GO again and choose Update from the drop-down menu.

In the Update Library Items dialog, note that it shows that 1 item needs to be updated.

With btn_GO checked in the Label column, choose Update.

Note that the dialog shows 1 item updated.

Choose Close to dismiss the dialog.

In the Library panel, select the symbol btn_GO.

In the Preview pane, note the updated appearance.

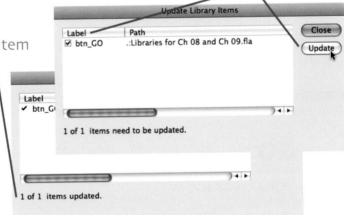

The btn_GO symbol and the other symbols you've imported are used throughout this chapter and they allow you to execute new, advanced tasks rather than spending time, and pages, repeating tasks you've already learned.

create input text

Text boxes in Flash are one of three types: static, dynamic, or input. So far, we've only worked with static text. We'll work with dynamic text later in this chapter; now we're going to create input text, meaning a text box for user input.

For our site, we'll add an input text field for users to enter their name. Then we'll add their name dynamically to some text, personalizing their experience.

In the Timeline, add a new layer above the layer site background and name it welcome.

In the Library, navigate to welcome input and text > gr_bkgdWelcome and drag an instance onto the gradient-filled rectangle, below the logo.

With the Free Transform tool, scale the width of the rectangle to match the logo tab above it.

Convert the selection to a symbol (F8). Name the symbol mc_welcomeMessage; then choose Movie Clip and center Registration.

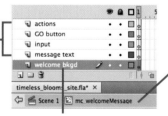

With the Selection tool, double-click the symbol to edit it.

In the Timeline, rename Layer 1 to welcome bkgd.

Insert four new layers in the Timeline. Name the layers as shown.

Select the layer message text.

From the Library panel, drag an instance of gr_request-Name onto the Stage, placing it over the background rectangle near the left edge. Use the arrow keys to nudge the text into place over the background.

create input text (cont.)

Select layer Go button and drag an instance of btn_Go onto the Stage, placing it near the right edge of the background rectangle. Use the arrow keys to nudge the button into place over the background.

In the Property Inspector, enter btnGO for the Instance Name.

Select layer input, choose the Text tool, and set these properties in the Property Inspector:

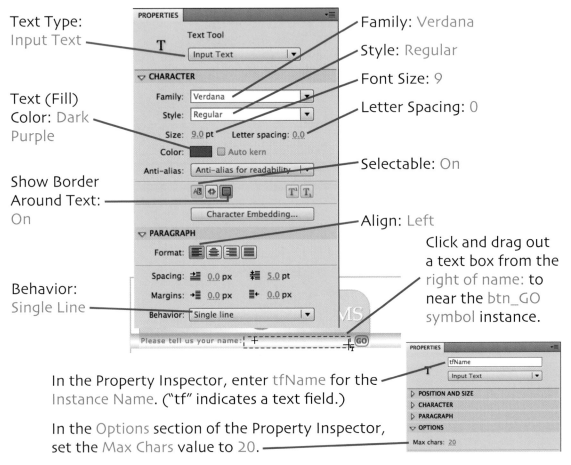

Text Type: Input Text

Text (Fill) Color: Dark Purple

Show Border Around Text: On

Behavior: Single Line

Family: Verdana

Style: Regular

Font Size: 9

Letter Spacing: 0

Selectable: On

Align: Left

Click and drag out a text box from the right of name: to near the btn_GO symbol instance.

In the Property Inspector, enter tfName for the Instance Name. ("tf" indicates a text field.)

In the Options section of the Property Inspector, set the Max Chars value to 20.

Choose the Selection tool to set the input text box. Use the Selection tool or arrow keys to adjust the placement of the text box.

set dynamic text

Test the movie. Click in the input field and enter your name to see that it does allow user input. Clicking the GO button doesn't do anything yet, but we'll set that up next.

First we need to set up an Action that will insert the user's name into a message, providing a personalized experience.

Close the Flash Player window.

Still in editing mode on the mc_welcome Message symbol, insert a keyframe in Frame 10 of all layers except the welcome bkgd layer.

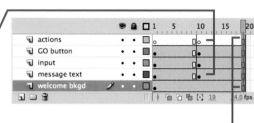

Insert a frame in Frame 19 of all the layers.

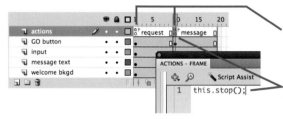

In the actions layer, label Frame 1 request and Frame 10 message.

In the Actions panel, add a stop command (this.stop();) in keyframes request and message.

In the keyframe message, delete the gr_requestName symbol instance, the input text box, and the btn_GO symbol.

Select keyframe message in layer message text.

Choose the Text tool.

In the Property Inspector, change the Text Type to Dynamic Text.

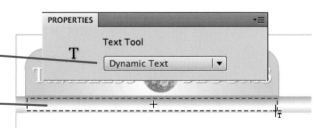

Click and drag out a text box from the left side of the background rectangle to the right edge.

set dynamic text (cont.)

With the Selection tool, select the dynamic text box.

Use the Selection tool or arrow keys to adjust the placement of the text box.

In the Property Inspector, enter tfMsg-Welcome for the Instance Name.

In the Character section, set Selectable and Show Border Around Text to off.

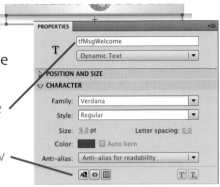

We have everything set up, now we just need to add the ActionScript to make it all work.

Select keyframe request in the actions layer.

In the Actions panel, enter the first piece of code as shown. Commented text, preceded by //, is not required; it provides some basic explanation of what the code does.

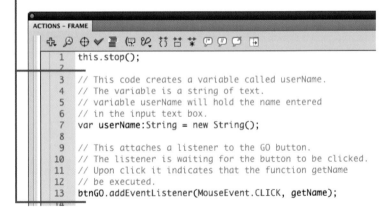

```
1   this.stop();
2
3   // This code creates a variable called userName.
4   // The variable is a string of text.
5   // variable userName will hold the name entered
6   // in the input text box.
7   var userName:String = new String();
8
9   // This attaches a listener to the GO button.
10  // The listener is waiting for the button to be clicked.
11  // Upon click it indicates that the function getName
12  // be executed.
13  btnGO.addEventListener(MouseEvent.CLICK, getName);
```

8 add inside sections of the web site

Now enter the second code section.

And finally, enter the third section.

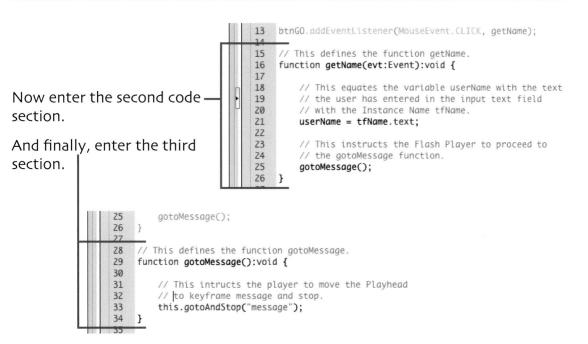

```
13   btnGO.addEventListener(MouseEvent.CLICK, getName);
14
15   // This defines the function getName.
16   function getName(evt:Event):void {
17
18      // This equates the variable userName with the text
19      // the user has entered in the input text field
20      // with the Instance Name tfName.
21      userName = tfName.text;
22
23      // This instructs the Flash Player to proceed to
24      // the gotoMessage function.
25      gotoMessage();
26   }
27
```

```
25      gotoMessage();
26   }
27
28   // This defines the function gotoMessage.
29   function gotoMessage():void {
30
31      // This intructs the player to move the Playhead
32      // to keyframe message and stop.
33      this.gotoAndStop("message");
34   }
35
```

Select keyframe message in the actions layer and enter the code in the Actions panel as shown. Type carefully. This won't work if there are any typos.

```
1   this.stop();
2
3   // This code puts together (concatenates in programming speak) the text
4   // between the first set of quotes, the value of the variable userName,
5   // and the text between the second set of quotes.
6   // It then assigns that text as the text in the tfMsgWelcome text box.
7   tfMsgWelcome.text ="Hello " + userName + ", welcome to Timeless Blooms";
```

Click Scene 1 in the Edit Bar to exit symbol-editing mode.

Test the movie.

Enter a name in the input text field and click the GO button.

Now you have a personalized message on your site greeting each visitor.

create scrolling text

Content for the Info section is contained in an HTML file that loads dynamically when our site movie is played. There's more text for the section than will fit within the content area of our layout, so to fit the text into the area we'll create a text box with an attached scroll bar component.

In the main file Timeline, select keyframe info in layer info content.

In the Library panel, open the bkgd Sections folder and drag out an instance of gr_bkgdInfo.

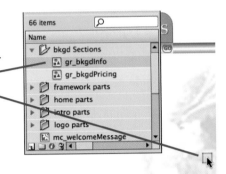

In the Position and Size section of the Property Inspector, set the position values to x = 20 and y = 110.

> **POSITION AND SIZE**
>
> X: 20.0   Y: 110.0
>
> W: 740.0   H: 465.0

Choose the Text tool.

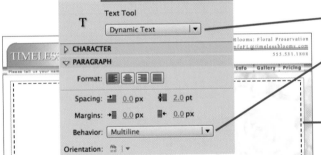

In the Property Inspector, set the Text Type to Dynamic Text and Behavior to Multiline.

Set line spacing to 2 pt. Click and drag out a text box near the size of the bkgd Content symbol.

Choose the Selection tool to set the text box.

With the text box selected, in the Character section of the Property Inspector, set Selectable to Off, Render Text as HTML to On, and Show Border Around Text to Off.

Choose Text > Scrollable to make the text box accept more text than will fit within its dimensions.

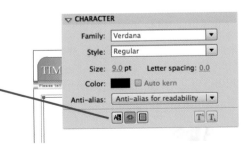

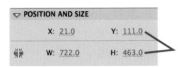

In the Property Inspector, unlink the width and height values and set the following values: X=21, Y=111, W=722, and H=463.

Convert the selected text box to a symbol.

Name the symbol mc_infoContent; choose Movie Clip and top-left Registration.

In the Property Inspector, name the instance contentInfo.

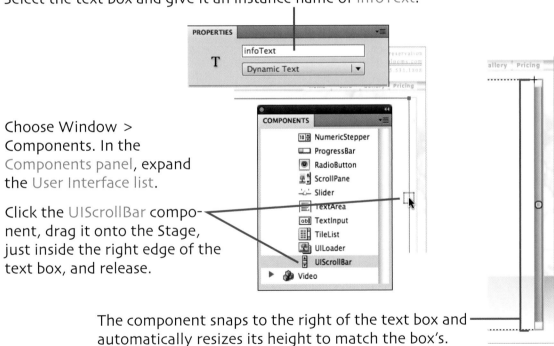

Double-click the symbol to edit it.

Select the text box and give it an instance name of infoText.

Choose Window > Components. In the Components panel, expand the User Interface list.

Click the UIScrollBar component, drag it onto the Stage, just inside the right edge of the text box, and release.

The component snaps to the right of the text box and automatically resizes its height to match the box's.

Give the UIScrollBar component an Instance Name of infoScroll.

With a scrolling text box created to contain it, we're ready to set up loading the HTML file containing the content for the Info section.

8 add inside sections of the web site   **105**

load and style html

The text-editing capabilities in Flash are best suited for small amounts like we've worked with so far. But for larger chunks of text it's often more efficient to keep the text in an external format that is loaded into the movie at runtime (when the movie plays in Flash Player). Placing text with simple HTML formatting in text (TXT) files makes updating the content much faster and easier—you can update the text file independent of your Flash movie.

Additionally, Cascading Style Sheets (CSS), used to define consistent appearances across sites, can be loaded into Flash to format text.

We'll place the ActionScript for loading a text file and a CSS file to style it in the Timeline of the mc_infoContent symbol.

Still in symbol-editing mode on the mc_infoContent symbol, insert a new layer and name it actions.

Select Keyframe 1 in the actions layer.

In the Actions panel enter the first section of code as shown. Commented text, preceded by //, is not required; it provides some basic explanation of what the code does.

```
1   // Create a string variable called userName.
2   var fileTxt:String;
3   // Create two variables named myTextLoader and cssLoader that load URLs.
4   var myTextLoader:URLLoader = new URLLoader();
5   var cssLoader:URLLoader = new URLLoader();
6   // Attach a listener to the myTextLoader URLLoader.
7   // The listener is waiting for the loader to complete loading of the url.
8   // Upon load completion it indicates that the function onLoaded be executed.
9   myTextLoader.addEventListener(Event.COMPLETE, onLoaded);
10  // Tell myTextLoader to load the textInfo.txt file.
11  myTextLoader.load(new URLRequest("textInfo.txt"));
12
13  // Define the function onLoaded.
14  function onLoaded(e:Event):void {
15      // Equate the variable fileTxt with the data (text)
16      // from the text file that myTextLoader has loaded.
17      fileTxt=myTextLoader.data;
18      // Instruct the Flash Player to proceed to the callCss function.
19      callCss();
20  }
```

8 add inside sections of the web site

Now enter the second code section.

```
        callCss();
    }

    // Define the function callCss.
    function callCss():void {
        // Create a variable cssRequest and request the file stylesSite.css.
        var cssRequest:URLRequest=new URLRequest("stylesSite.css");
        // Attach a listener to the cssRequest URLRequest.
        // The listener is waiting for the loader to complete loading of the url.
        // Upon load completion it indicates that the function onCss be executed.
        cssLoader.addEventListener(Event.COMPLETE, onCss);
        // Tell variable cssLoader to load the contents of the css file.
        cssLoader.load(cssRequest);
    }
```

And finally, enter the third section.

```
        cssLoader.load(cssRequest);
    }

    // Define the function onCss.
    function onCss(e:Event):void {
        // Create a StyleSheet variable named css.
        var css:StyleSheet = new StyleSheet();
        // Tell the css StyleSheet variable to parse the css that cssLoader loaded
        css.parseCSS(cssLoader.data);
        // Apply the css styleSheet to our infoText text box.
        // Turn on word wrapping in the infoText text box.
        // Fill the infoText text box with the text from the variable fileTxt.
        infoText.styleSheet=css;
        infoText.wordWrap=true;
        infoText.htmlText=fileTxt;
        // Update the scroll bar component infoScroll to make it aware of the text
        //now in the text box so that it will be active.
        infoScroll.update();
    }
```

You can use this code in your own projects, just remember to change the references to "infoText" to match the instance name you give your target text box. Also change "textInfo.txt" and "stylesSite.css" to match the names of your files.

8 add inside sections of the web site

load and style html (cont.)

Select Scene 1 in the Edit Bar to exit symbol-editing mode.

Test the movie, [Ctrl][⏎ Enter] (Windows) or [⌘][⏎ Enter] (Mac).

Click the Info button, and you'll see that not only is the text box populated with the contents of the text file, including an image linked from within the HTML, but also the text is formatted nicely.

Our Info section is now complete!

Close the Flash Player and save your Flash file.

In order to decrease the initial download time when a user visits a site, we can create content in separate Flash movies that load into the main movie as viewers move through the site. We'll work an example of that technique next.

8 add inside sections of the web site

load xml content

For our Gallery slide show, we'll create a movie that builds its interface on the fly by parsing an XML file. Maintaining descriptions of content in a separate file makes it easy to add and remove examples without editing and republishing the Flash movie. The Flash movie we'll publish will use ActionScript 2.0, a previous version of the scripting language, to give us access to several features that are useful to the Flash beginner. (See extra bits on page 125.)

Let's take a quick look at the XML file we'll use.

Choose File > Open.

In the Open dialog, navigate to the development_files directory. Change the Files of Type menu to All Files (*.*) (Windows) or All Formats (Mac).

Select the file dataGallery.xml and click Open.

Without getting into the details of XML formatting, you should be able to discern the following:

The file contains a series of entries in the top-level category of displays, <displays>.

Within the displays category there are four second-level groups, called nodes, [n], in XML, for display types, <type>. Each type has a name attribute.

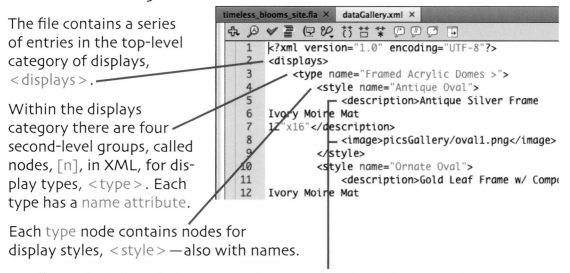

Each type node contains nodes for display styles, <style>—also with names.

Finally, each style node has two nodes nested within it for descriptions and images.

With that basic understanding, we're ready to work on the Flash movie that will use the XML.

load xml content (cont.)

Open the file galleryContent.fla. To speed our task, the file already has four named layers and a background layout upon which we'll build the gallery.

Select the layer xml connector.

In the Components panel, note the presence of a Data category that was not available to us in our main file that uses ActionScript 3.0. Open the Data list, drag out an instance of XML Connector, and place it off the left edge of the Stage.

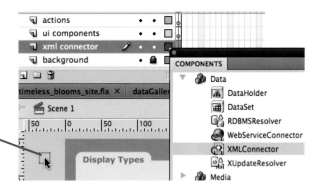

The XML Connector serves as a go-between, bringing data in from the XML file and broadcasting out to UI components that use the data to determine their displays.

Although it would not be visible in the movie if placed on the Stage, it's common to place it just off the top-left corner so it doesn't cause visual clutter or interfere with access to other objects in your document.

In the Property Inspector, give the component an Instance Name of xcGallery.

Choose Window > Component Inspector and set the following values:

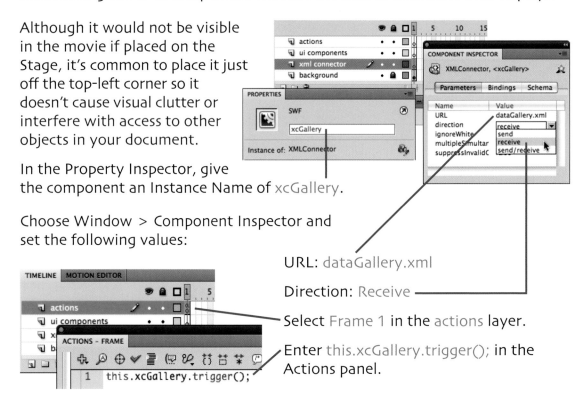

URL: dataGallery.xml

Direction: Receive

Select Frame 1 in the actions layer.

Enter this.xcGallery.trigger(); in the Actions panel.

Select the XML Cap Connector xcGallery.

In the Component Inspector, click the Schema tab.

In the scroll pane, select results : XML.

Click the Import a schema from a sample XML file button in the upper-right corner of the Schema tab.

In the Open dialog, select dataGallery.xml and click Open.

Expand your view of the scroll pane to see the additions to the results: XML section.

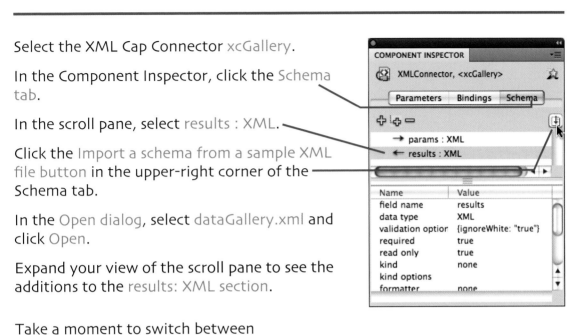

Take a moment to switch between galleryContent.fla and dataGallery.xml to see how the tag structures in the XML are parsed into the hierarchical data properties in the Schema tab.

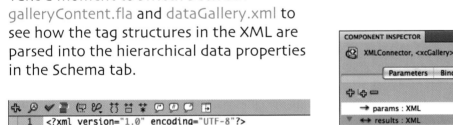

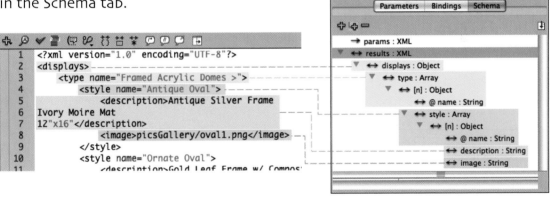

Close the file dataGallery.xml.

Save the file galleryContent.fla.

We have the process in place to import the XML. Now let's set up a user interface to use it.

use ui components

Select the layer ui components.

From the Components panel User Interface list, drag an instance of the List component onto the Stage. Place it on the green background below the Display Types heading.

In the Property Inspector, set these values:

Instance Name: listDisplays

X: 25

Y: 40

W: 145

H: 80

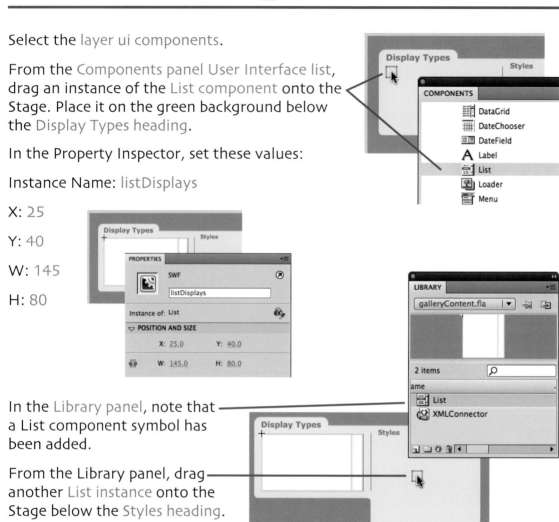

In the Library panel, note that a List component symbol has been added.

From the Library panel, drag another List instance onto the Stage below the Styles heading.

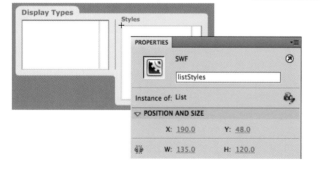

Give the List the Instance Name of listStyles, location of X: 190 and Y: 48, and dimensions of W: 135 X H: 120.

Next, drag an instance of the TextArea component from the Components panel, placing it over the light purple background.

Set properties to an Instance Name of descStyles, X: 120 and Y: 250, and W: 205 X H: 75.

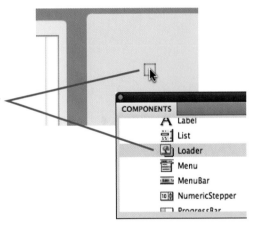

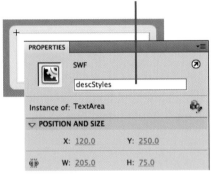

Finally, drag an instance of the Loader component onto the light gray background.

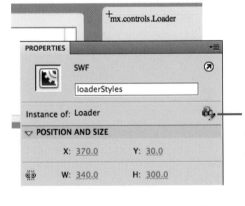

Set properties to an Instance Name of loaderStyles, X: 370 and Y: 30, and W: 340 X H: 300.

OK, now we have an XML file providing data, an XML Connector to import and distribute the data, and user interface elements ready to be driven by the data. We just need to establish all the connections.

bind data to the ui

When we connect a piece of data from an XML file to a user interface element, it's known as binding the data. Binding each piece of data to a component via the XML Connector is a multistep process. We bind the data to the XML Connector and specify to which UI component the connector will broadcast the data. Then we bind the incoming data to the component and specify how it will be handled.

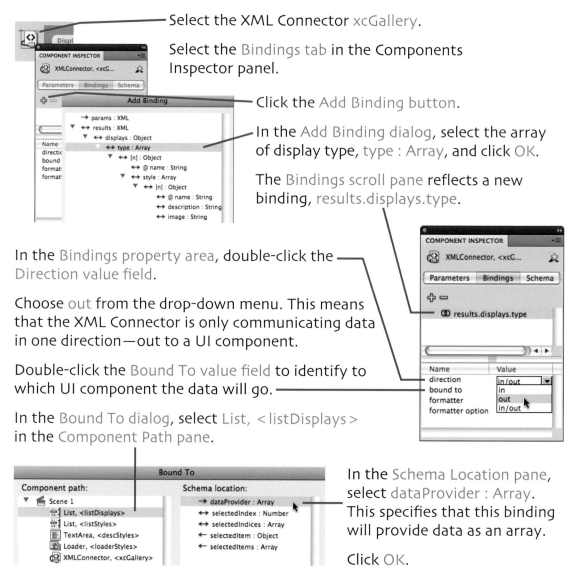

Select the XML Connector xcGallery.

Select the Bindings tab in the Components Inspector panel.

Click the Add Binding button.

In the Add Binding dialog, select the array of display type, type : Array, and click OK.

The Bindings scroll pane reflects a new binding, results.displays.type.

In the Bindings property area, double-click the Direction value field.

Choose out from the drop-down menu. This means that the XML Connector is only communicating data in one direction—out to a UI component.

Double-click the Bound To value field to identify to which UI component the data will go.

In the Bound To dialog, select List, < listDisplays > in the Component Path pane.

In the Schema Location pane, select dataProvider : Array. This specifies that this binding will provide data as an array.

Click OK.

Next, we'll repeat the bindings process for the style node and the two style objects—description and image.

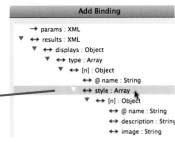

With the XML Connector still selected, click the Add Binding button.

Select style : Array and click OK.

A new binding, results.displays.type.[n].style, is listed in the panel.

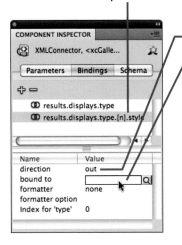

Set the Direction value to out.

Double-click the Bound To value field.

In the Bound To dialog, select:

Component Path: List, < listStyles >

Schema Location: dataProvider : Array

Click OK.

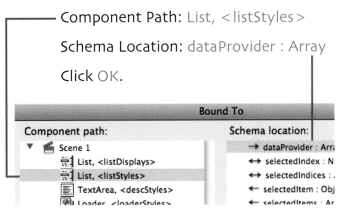

Repeat the steps to create these two bindings:

1 Binding to: description : String

Direction: out

Bound To:

Component Path: TextArea, < descStyles >

Schema Location: text : String

bind data to the ui (cont.)

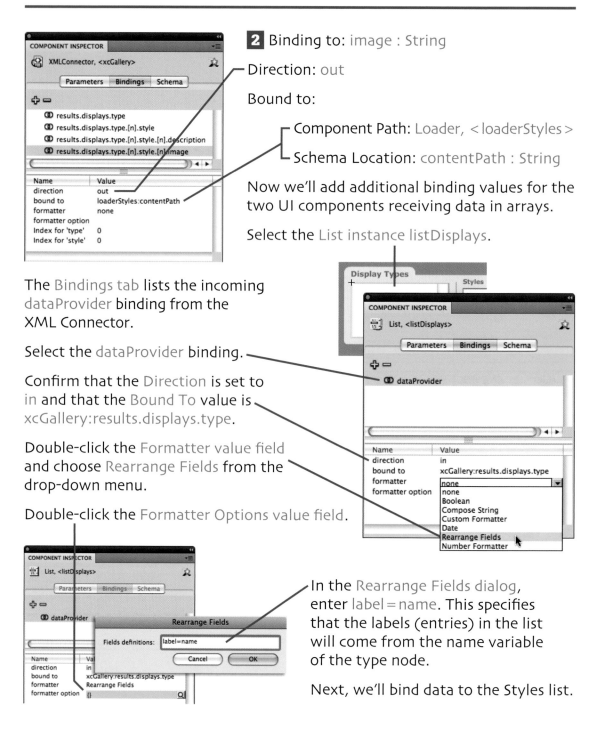

2 Binding to: image : String

Direction: out

Bound to:

Component Path: Loader, <loaderStyles>

Schema Location: contentPath : String

Now we'll add additional binding values for the two UI components receiving data in arrays.

Select the List instance listDisplays.

The Bindings tab lists the incoming dataProvider binding from the XML Connector.

Select the dataProvider binding.

Confirm that the Direction is set to in and that the Bound To value is xcGallery:results.displays.type.

Double-click the Formatter value field and choose Rearrange Fields from the drop-down menu.

Double-click the Formatter Options value field.

In the Rearrange Fields dialog, enter label=name. This specifies that the labels (entries) in the list will come from the name variable of the type node.

Next, we'll bind data to the Styles list.

Select the List instance listStyles.

In the Bindings panel, Select the dataProvider binding.

Confirm Direction is in and Bound To is xcGallery:results.displays.type.[n].style.

Double-click the Formatter value field and choose Rearrange Fields from the drop-down menu.

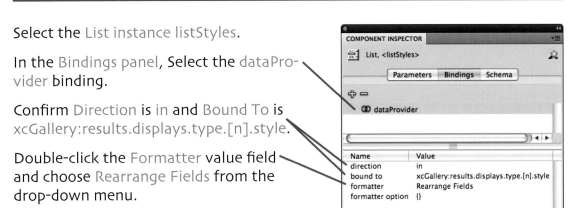

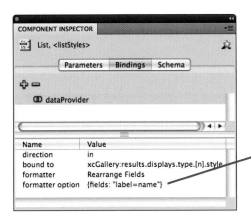

Double-click the Formatter Options value field, and enter label = name in the Rearrange Fields dialog.

Let's take a look at what we've done so far.

Test the movie, [Ctrl][↵Enter] (Windows) or [⌘][↵Enter] (Mac).

All of our UI elements are now displaying content. It's a great start, but there's no connection between the elements and no response to making a selection in one of the lists.

We'll change that next.

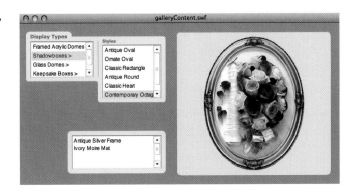

set ui interactions

For our UI to function correctly, we need the Styles list to respond to selections in the Display Types list and for the description and image to respond to selections in the Styles list. We'll set up these interactions now.

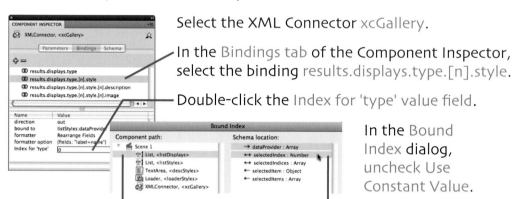

Select the XML Connector xcGallery.

In the Bindings tab of the Component Inspector, select the binding results.displays.type.[n].style.

Double-click the Index for 'type' value field.

In the Bound Index dialog, uncheck Use Constant Value.

Select List, <listDisplays> in the Component Path pane and selectedIndex : Number in the Schema Location pane.

Click OK.

In the Component Inspector, confirm that the Index for 'type' value shows listDisplays:selectedIndex.

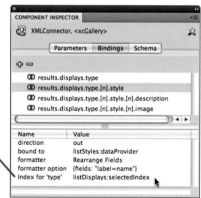

This has bound listStyles to the selection in listDisplays.

Select the binding results.displays.type.[n].style.[n].description.

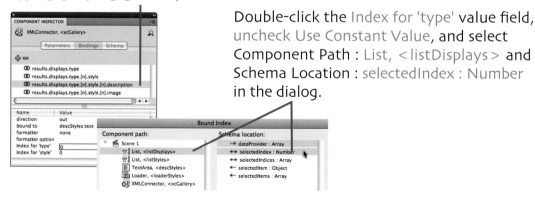

Double-click the Index for 'type' value field, uncheck Use Constant Value, and select Component Path : List, <listDisplays> and Schema Location : selectedIndex : Number in the dialog.

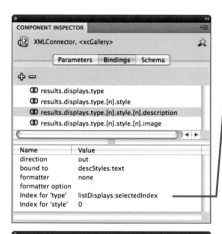

Confirm that the Index for 'type' value is set to listDisplays:selected Index.

Double-click the Index for 'style' value field, uncheck Use Constant Value, and select Component Path : List, < listStyles > and Schema Location : selectedIndex : Number in the dialog.

Click OK.

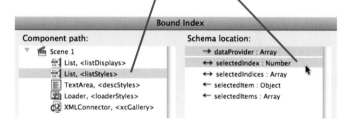

Confirm that the Index for 'style' value is set to listStyles:selected Index.

Select the binding results.displays.type.[n]. style.[n].image.

Repeat the previous steps to:

Set the Index for 'type' value to listDisplays: selected Index

Set the Index for 'style' value to listStyles: selected Index.

Finally, we need to specify the default values for the two List instances.

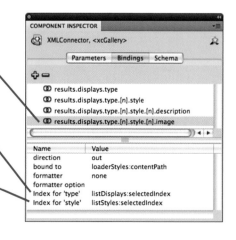

set ui interactions (cont.)

Select the List instance listDisplays.

Select the Schema tab in the Component Inspector panel.

Select the selectedIndex : Number property.

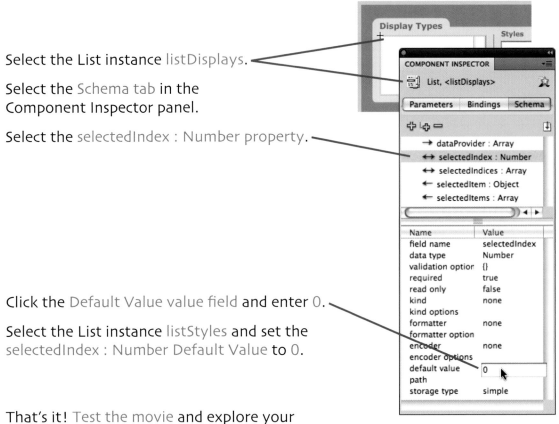

Click the Default Value value field and enter 0.

Select the List instance listStyles and set the selectedIndex : Number Default Value to 0.

That's it! Test the movie and explore your fully functioning Displays Gallery.

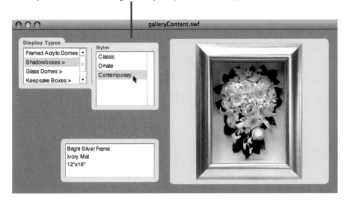

Close the Flash Player window.

When we test a movie, Flash exports a SWF movie file to play in the Flash Player, placing it in the same directory as the Flash file. Since we have no special publishing requirements for this movie, we can use that SWF to load into our main movie.

Save the Flash file galleryContent.fla.

load external movies

Back in our main Flash file (timeless_blooms_site.fla), we need to set up the file to load the galleryContent.swf movie into the Gallery section.

Select the keyframe gallery in the gallery content layer.

2 In the Property Inspector, name the symbol instance loaderGallery. Set the position X: 20 and Y: 115.

1 From the Components panel, drag an instance of the UILoader component onto the Stage.

3 In the Component Inspector, click the source value field and enter galleryContent.swf. If our main SWF movie and galleryContent.swf were to be located in different directories, the path would be more complex from one to the other.

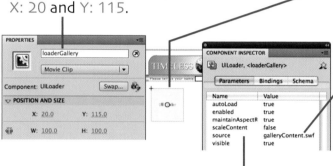

4 Double-click the scaleContent parameter value field, and select false in the drop-down menu. This instructs Flash to display our movie at its actual size, not sizing it to the 100 X 100 dimensions of the Loader symbol.

Choose Control > Test Movie, or press Ctrl +←Enter (Windows) or ⌘ ←Enter (Mac). When the movie appears in the Flash Player window, click the Gallery button.

You see that our contentGallery movie with its XML-driven gallery is displayed in the content area exactly as we wanted.

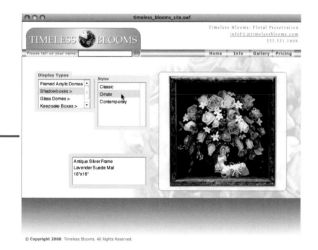

Close the Flash Player window.

That's it. Our Gallery section is created and fully functional within our main site movie.

form components

Forms provide a common function in Web pages, providing a way for users to interact with the businesses and people behind a site. For our Pricing section, we will create the basic framework of a form using components. To function properly and transfer data as intended, a form requires advanced ActionScript programming and connection to a database—complexity that is beyond the scope of this book. We'll limit our exercise to establishing the basics.

Select keyframe Pricing in the pricing content layer.

From the Library panel, drag out an instance of the symbol bkgd Sections > gr_bkgdPricing. Again, to speed our task, the symbol already has three named layers and a background layout upon which we'll place the form objects.

Position the symbol at X: 20 and Y: 115.

Double-click the bkgdPricing instance to invoke symbol-editing mode.

Select the ui components layer.

From the Components panel, drag out an instance of the TextInput component. Place the instance next to the label Name.

Name the instance inputName.

Confirm that the Width and Height values are unlinked, and set the width to 220 px.

Drag out another TextInput instance, placing it next to E-mail Address.

Name the instance inputEmail and set the width to 220 px.

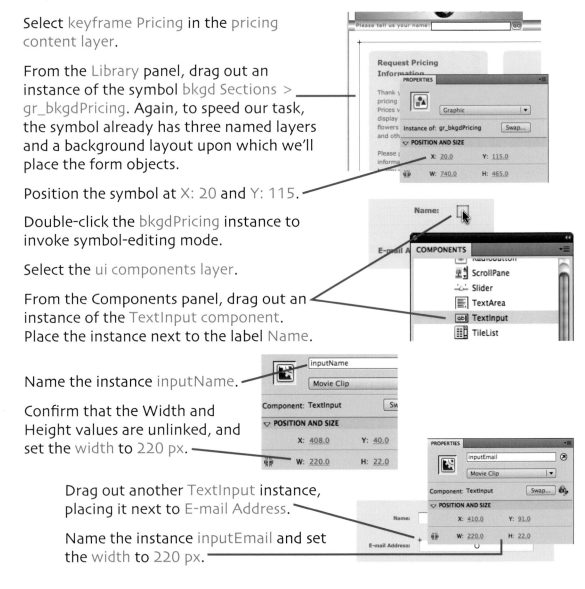

Drag out an instance of the RadioButton component, and place it next to Event.

Name the instance radioWedding.

In the Component Inspector panel, click to select the groupName parameter and enter groupEvent, identifying this radio button as part of a group containing other radio buttons we haven't yet placed.

Click to select the label parameter, and enter Wedding.

Choose true from the selected parameter drop-down menu.

Drag out another RadioButton instance to the right of the Wedding RadioButton.

Set the Instance Name to radioProm, groupName to groupEvent, and label to Jr. / Sr. Prom.

Place another RadioButton instance below Wedding and name it radioAnniversary. Set groupName to groupEvent and label to Anniversary Party.

Change the width to 120 to show the entire label.

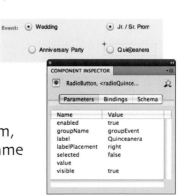

Place a final RadioButton below Jr. / Sr. Prom, and name it radioQuinceanera. Set groupName to groupEvent and label to Quinceanera.

form components (cont.)

Drag an instance of the ComboBox component below the display type statement.

Name the instance comboDisplay and set the width to 155.

Double-click the dataProvider value field.

In the dialog, click the Add New Value button four times.

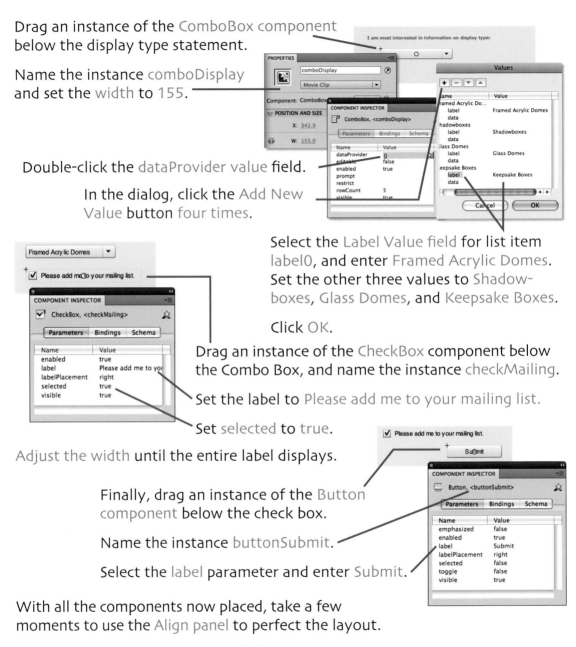

Select the Label Value field for list item label0, and enter Framed Acrylic Domes. Set the other three values to Shadowboxes, Glass Domes, and Keepsake Boxes.

Click OK.

Drag an instance of the CheckBox component below the Combo Box, and name the instance checkMailing.

Set the label to Please add me to your mailing list.

Set selected to true.

Adjust the width until the entire label displays.

Finally, drag an instance of the Button component below the check box.

Name the instance buttonSubmit.

Select the label parameter and enter Submit.

With all the components now placed, take a few moments to use the Align panel to perfect the layout.

Test the Movie and see how the different components operate.

Close the Flash Player. That's it for our inside sections.

extra bits

load xml content p. 109

ActionScript 2.0 is an older version of the ActionScript language that was the standard bearer until ActionScript 3.0 (AS3) was introduced with Adobe Flash CS3 Professional. While AS3 was a giant step forward in making ActionScript a more robust programming language that would appeal to the needs of programmers and help to expand the capabilities of the Flash platform into more application-type uses, it also became much harder for the novice user to learn and use. Additionally, features that were available within Flash made simple (and sometimes not-so-simple) interactivity easier for the novice to achieve. Features such as the Behaviors panel and the XML components are no longer available when working with an AS3 document.

For our project, we use AS3 in the main site file for the simple tasks of stopping the Timeline or acting on mouse clicks and moving the Timeline accordingly. However, given the scope and brevity of this book, achieving the Gallery of images is not feasible using AS3.

To provide the reader with a way to achieve some of the more complex tasks, such as the XML connectivity we do here, that were easier in AS2,

we are taking advantage of a nice feature available in the Flash Player.

While it is not possible to mix ActionScript 2.0 and ActionScript 3.0 in the same Flash file, the Flash Player is capable of playing an AS2 file and an AS3 file at the same time, even when one of the files is loaded into the other. That's why for our Gallery we work with an AS2 file, galleryContent.fla, and take advantage of the XML Connector and all the functionality it provides through the Component Inspector panel to establish the links between the data in the XML file and the UI Components on our Stage.

9. use flash video

Video is one of the most popular trends on the Web, and Flash offers truly unmatched video capabilities. Many of the most well-known sites offering video use the Flash Player for delivery because of the compression available in the Flash Video (FLV) format, the flexibility of playback controls, and the ability to synch events in a Flash movie with points in the video files.

In this chapter you'll learn to:

Listen for cue point triggers to execute other actions in the Flash movie.

Use named cue points to dynamically alter text.

Use Adobe Media Encoder CS4 to convert videos to the Flash Video format.

Use ActionScript to dynamically change the visibility of objects.

Use ActionScript with buttons to navigate to cue points in the video.

127

video playback area

Our video will display in a "video screen" area made visible with the click of a button. Before we import the video, we'll lay out the video screen and set up the button interaction.

In the main Timeline of timeless_blooms_site.fla, add a new layer above layer buttons. Name the new layer video.

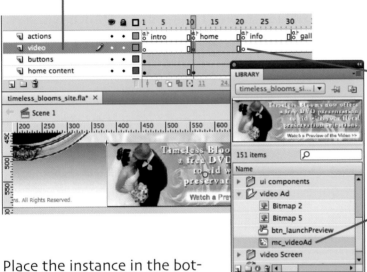

Select Keyframe home in layer video and insert a keyframe (F6).

Select Keyframe info and insert a keyframe.

Click back in Keyframe home.

From the Library panel, drag out an instance of symbol mc_videoAd from the video Ad folder.

Place the instance in the bottom-right corner of the Stage.

In the Property Inspector, name the instance videoAd.

Drag an instance of symbol mc_videoScreen from the video Screen folder. The basic elements of the video screen have been laid out in advance, allowing us to concentrate on video tasks.

Name the instance videoScreen.

In the Position and Size section of the Property Inspector, enter X: 0.0 and Y: 95.0.

The mc_videoScreen symbol will not be visible when our Web site first loads. Viewers will click a button in mc_videoAd to see it. Let's set up that action now.

In the Timeline, select Keyframe home in the actions layer.

Below the stop action, enter the code as shown to make the video screen invisible when the frame loads.

```
this.stop()

// Make the videoScreen instance invisible.
videoScreen.visible=false;
```

Double-click the symbol instance mc_videoAd to invoke symbol-editing mode.

Click the text Watch a Preview of the Video >> to select the symbol btn_launchPreview.

Name the instance btnLaunch.

In the Library panel, double-click the symbol icon for mc_videoScreen to invoke symbol-editing mode.

Select the symbol instance btn_videoClose in the top-right corner.

Name the instance btnClose.

Click Scene 1 in the Edit Bar to exit symbol-editing mode and select Keyframe home in the actions layer.

```
// Make the videoScreen instance invisible.
videoScreen.visible=false;

// Add a listener object to the btnLaunch instance.
// Execute function showScreen on click.
videoAd.btnLaunch.addEventListener(MouseEvent.CLICK, showScreen);
// Define function showScreen.
function showScreen(evt:Event):void {
    // Make the videoScreen instance visible.
    videoScreen.visible=true;
}
// Add a listener object to the btnClose instance.
// Execute function hideScreen on click.
videoScreen.btnClose.addEventListener(MouseEvent.CLICK, hideScreen);
// Define function hideScreen.
function hideScreen(evt:Event):void {
    // Stop video playback.
    videoScreen.theVideo.stop();
    // Make the videoScreen instance invisible.
    videoScreen.visible=false;
}
```

In the Actions panel, enter the code as shown to enable the buttons to open and close the video screen and stop video playback.

Note that if our video had audio and we didn't stop playback, the video would continue to play and viewers would still hear the audio when the video disappeared.

9 use flash video 129

import video

With our video screen layout in place, we're ready to bring in our video file. But first we need to convert it to the Flash Video (FLV) format. We also want to insert cue points—markers that start other actions in the Flash movie and let us synchronize other content with the video playback. We'll convert our video file and add cue points using Adobe Media Encoder CS4.

Double-click the mc_videoScreen symbol instance to invoke symbol-editing mode. Select layer video in the Timeline.

Select File > Import > Import Video to launch the Flash Video Import Wizard.

In the Select Video pane, click the Launch Adobe Media Encoder button.

Read the Message dialog and click OK as Adobe Media Encoder CS4 opens.

2 Navigate to the development_files folder. Select videoWedding.mp4 and click Open.

1 In the encoder pane, click Add.

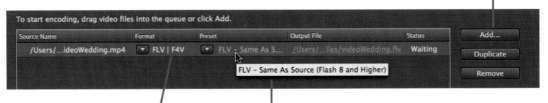

3 In the Format column, select FLV | F4V from the drop-down menu.

4 In the Preset column, select FLV - Same as Source (Flash 8 and Higher).

Choose Edit > Export Settings.

In the Export Settings dialog, click the Add Cue Point button.

In the Cue Point Name column, click the text Cue Point and change it to The Bride and Groom.

In the Type drop-down menu, select Navigation.

Enter cue point names carefully; they must match exactly some frame labels in a Movie Clip symbol that we'll work with shortly.

Click and drag the Playback Head to the right, progressing through the video. Just past the 8-second mark, there is an edit switching from the bride and groom to a clip of the bouquet toss.

Release the Playback Head as close to the edit as you can. Use the left and right arrow keys on your keyboard to more precisely place the Playback Head at the edit.

Click the Add Cue Point button and enter The Toss as the Name. Set the Type to Navigation.

Drag the Playback Head further until you see the bouquet toss dissolve to the couple kissing.

Click the Add Cue Point button and enter The Kiss as the Name. Set the Type to Navigation.

Finally, move the Playback Head to the point where that clip dissolves to wedding rings.

Add a cue point named The Rings, with Type set to Navigation.

Click OK to close the Export Settings dialog.

In the Output File column of the encoder pane, confirm the output path leads to the development_ files folder and the file will be named videoWedding.flv.

Choose Start Queue.

When the conversion is complete, Quit the Adobe Media Encoder CS4 application and switch back to the Flash Video Import Wizard.

import video (cont.)

In the Select Video pane, click the Browse button under the On your computer selection and navigate to the development_files folder. Select videoWedding.flv and click Open.

Back in the Select Video pane, confirm that Load external video with playback component is selected. Click Continue.

In the Skinning pane, we choose the control types and appearance attached to the video. From the Skin drop-down menu, choose SkinUnderAllNoVolNoCaptionNoFull.swf for controls outside the video with all controls except volume, captions, and full screen view.

Set Color to our light green.

Click Continue.

Read the messages in the Finish Video Import pane and click Finish.

Wait as Flash adds the playback controls and attaches the movie to an FLVPlayback component.

Click in the black area of the FLVPlayback component and drag, placing it just below the green shaded tab.

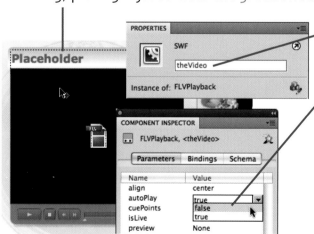

Name the instance theVideo.

In the Component Inspector, set the autoPlay value to false.

Test your movie. From the Home section, click the button in the ad to open the video screen and watch the video play.

Close the Flash Player.

use cue points

Examine the different elements in the mc_videoScreen symbol.

The Dynamic text box named tfHeader will display cue point names as the video plays.

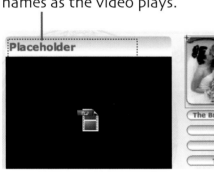

The movie clip instance of symbol mc_video-Banner, named mcVideoBanner, has four keyframes with frame labels that match exactly the cue point names. Cue points will trigger moves between the keyframes.

The four buttons will move the video playhead to the matching cue points.

To respond to the cue points in the video, we'll set up ActionScript "listeners" that will listen for the cue points and then execute actions we specify.

Click Scene 1 in the Edit Bar to exit symbol-editing mode.

Select Keyframe home in the layer actions.

In the Actions panel, before the code this.stop(), enter the code as shown here.

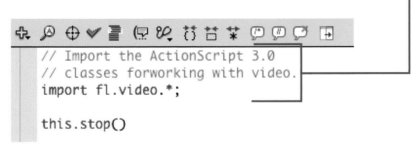

```
// Import the ActionScript 3.0
// classes forworking with video.
import fl.video.*;

this.stop()
```

use cue points (cont.)

Scroll the Actions panel and place the code shown here after the code for function hideScreen.

```
                // Make the videoScreen instance invisible.
            videoScreen.visible=false;
        }

        // Add a listener object to the instance theVideo inside the instance videoScreen.
        // Execute function cuePointListener when a cue point is encountered by the Playhead.
        videoScreen.theVideo.addEventListener(MetadataEvent.CUE_POINT, cuePointListener);
        // Define function cuePointListener
        function cuePointListener(event:MetadataEvent):void {
            // Assign the name of the encountered cue point as the value of variable cueName.
            var cueName=event.info.name;
            // Assign the value of cueName as the text in text
            // field tfHeader inside the instance videoScreen.
            videoScreen.tfHeader.text=cueName;
            // Move the Playhead in the movie clip mcVideoBanner inside the instance
            // videoScreen to the frame label that matches the value of cueName.
            videoScreen.mcVideoBanner.gotoAndStop(cueName);
        }
```

Script

Test your movie. From the Home section, click the button in the ad to open the video screen, and click the Play button to watch the video.

Note that the header text Placeholder in text box tfHeader is replaced by the cue point names as the video plays past each cue point.

Also note that the banner graphic changes, indicating the Playhead has moved to another labeled keyframe.

Close the Flash Player.

9 use flash video

Now let's add ActionScript to enable the buttons for viewers to navigate to the points in the video. In the mc_videoScreen symbol, the button symbol instance with the text The Bride and Groom is named btnBandG. The other three button instances are named similarly—btnToss, btnKiss, and btnRings.

With Keyframe home in the layer actions selected, enter the code as shown here in the Actions panel after the code for function cuePointListener.

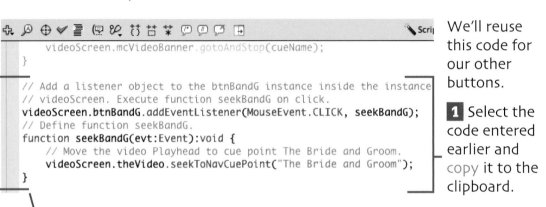

```
        videoScreen.mcVideoBanner.gotoAndStop(cueName);
    }

// Add a listener object to the btnBandG instance inside the instance
// videoScreen. Execute function seekBandG on click.
videoScreen.btnBandG.addEventListener(MouseEvent.CLICK, seekBandG);
// Define function seekBandG.
function seekBandG(evt:Event):void {
    // Move the video Playhead to cue point The Bride and Groom.
    videoScreen.theVideo.seekToNavCuePoint("The Bride and Groom");
}
```

We'll reuse this code for our other buttons.

1 Select the code entered earlier and copy it to the clipboard.

2 Paste the code after the last line of code in the pane. You need to make four important changes to make this code control another button.

3 In the first line, change videoScreen.btnBandG to videoScreen.btnToss and the function from seekBandG to seekToss.

4 In the second line, change the function from seekBandG to seekToss.

```
        videoScreen.theVideo.seekToNavCuePoint("The Bride and Groom");
    }

videoScreen.btnToss.addEventListener(MouseEvent.CLICK, seekToss);
function seekToss(evt:Event):void {
    videoScreen.theVideo.seekToNavCuePoint("The Toss");
}
```

5 Finally, in the last line, change the cue point name from "The Bride and Groom" to "The Toss". Remember that you must enter this name exactly as you did when naming the cue points in Adobe Media Encoder CS4.

use cue points (cont.)

Paste the code again and repeat steps 1-5 for the button The Kiss using btnKiss and seekKiss in step 3; seekKiss in step 4; and "The Kiss" in step 5.

```
        videoScreen.theVideo.seekToNavCuePoint("The Toss");
    }

    videoScreen.btnKiss.addEventListener(MouseEvent.CLICK, seekKiss);
    function seekKiss(evt:Event):void {
        videoScreen.theVideo.seekToNavCuePoint("The Kiss");
    }

    videoScreen.btnRings.addEventListener(MouseEvent.CLICK, seekRings);
    function seekRings(evt:Event):void {
        videoScreen.theVideo.seekToNavCuePoint("The Rings");
    }
```

Repeat the process for the button The Rings.

Test your movie. From the Home section, click the button in the ad to open the video screen. Randomly click the buttons to move the Playback Head among the different cue points.

Click the Play button to start video playback and click the buttons randomly.

That's it! You've successfully imported Flash video, embedded cue points, and used those cue points to trigger ActionScript events and as navigation targets.

Close the Flash Player.

Our site development is complete, and we're ready to publish to the Web!

10. publish your web site

With development of all our site sections complete, the only thing left to do is to ready our files for upload to the Web.

In this chapter we accomplish the following:

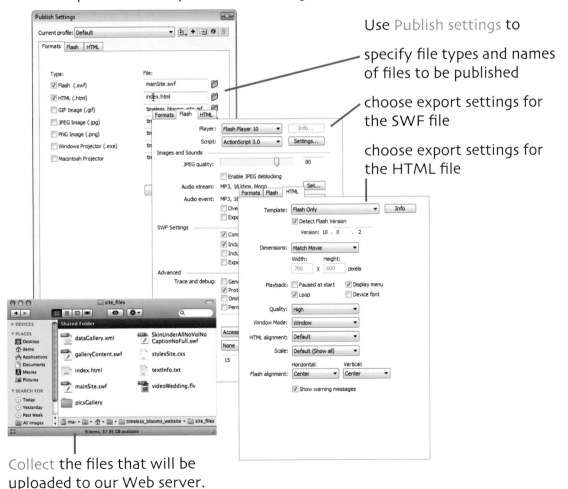

Use Publish settings to

specify file types and names of files to be published

choose export settings for the SWF file

choose export settings for the HTML file

Collect the files that will be uploaded to our Web server.

swf settings

In Flash, we have the opportunity to specify different attributes for the files we're going to publish. In this section, we'll determine the Publish Settings for our main site movie.

Choose File > Publish Settings, or click the Edit button next to Profile in the Publish section of the Property Inspector. The Publish Settings dialog appears.

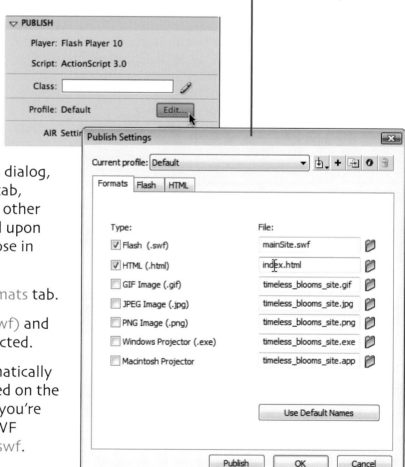

In the Publish Settings dialog, there is one constant tab, Formats, and multiple other tabs that appear based upon the file types you choose in the Formats tab.

Click to select the Formats tab.

Confirm that Flash (.swf) and HTML (.html) are selected.

Note that Flash automatically assigns file names based on the name of the Flash file you're editing. Change the SWF file name to mainSite.swf.

Change the HTML file name to index.html.

Click the Flash tab. The Player drop-down menu defaults to the Flash Player version associated with the version of Flash you're using. In our case, that's Flash Player 10.

Leave Script set to ActionScript 3.0.

In the Images and Sounds section, set JPEG Quality to 80.

Leave Enable JPEG Deblocking unchecked, we don't need it with JPEG Quality set at 80.

Our one sound file was optimized before import, so we don't need to change anything in the Audio settings.

In the SWF Settings section, choose Compress Movie to reduce file size and Include Hidden Layers, in case you accidentally left visibility of a layer off as you worked.

Uncheck Include XMP Metadata; we didn't use that feature.

Uncheck Export SWC.

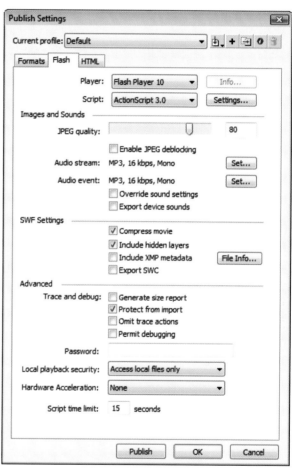

In the Advanced section, select Protect from Import to prevent other people from importing your SWF file into Flash—protecting your work from theft. Uncheck the other options.

Leave the Password field blank.

Set Local Playback Security to Access Local Files Only.

Set Hardware Acceleration to None.

Leave the Script Time Limit value at 15.

html settings

Flash movies on the Web need to be embedded in HTML files that provide movie display instructions to the browser. The HTML files can also include code that checks for the presence of the correct Flash Player plug-in and redirects the viewer if it's not there.

Luckily, Flash can publish the HTML code we need so we don't have to do the coding.

Select the HTML tab.

Flash generates the HTML file from a set of customizable templates designed for different Flash delivery requirements.

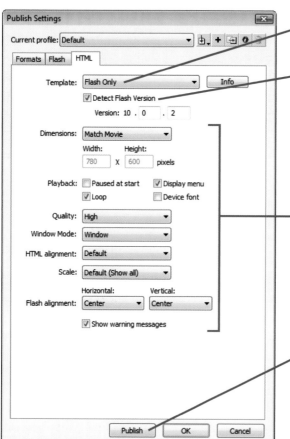

Choose Flash Only from the Template drop-down menu.

We want our file to test for the Flash plug-in and to provide an opportunity to install it if it isn't present. Click the check box to select Detect Flash Version. The values for Version will set automatically.

The remaining options in the HTML tab allow users to customize how their movies appear and behave in the browser window. For our purposes, the default settings are appropriate, so we won't make any changes.

Click the Publish button to generate the SWF movie file and the HTML file we've requested.

Click OK to close the dialog.

Save and close any files open in Flash. Choose File > Exit (Windows) or Flash > Quit Flash (Mac) to close the Flash application.

From your computer's desktop, navigate to the development_files folder. You'll see that Flash has added the Flash movie (mainSite.swf) and the HTML file (index.html).

Double-click the file index.html to open it in the browser.

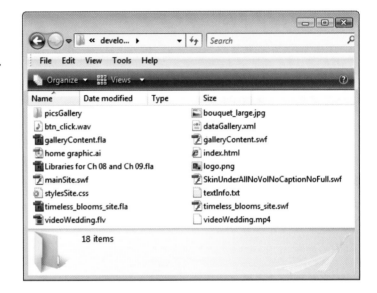

Because you have the correct plug-in (that was installed with the Flash application), you will see our completed site movie displayed. If you didn't have the plug-in, you would see alternative content with instructions to download it.

collect files for upload

Our final step is to collect all the files that will be uploaded to your Web server and copy them into the site_files folder. The following is a list of the files to copy, along with brief descriptions:

galleryContent.swf—Gallery section movie that includes XML parsing and bindings

dataGallery.xml—XML file that includes all the tags describing items in the gallery

index.html— Page containing mainSite.swf; our site is displayed in this page; executes Flash Player detection and redirects, if necessary

mainSite.swf—our main site movie including the Home section, animated intro, inside sections, and video

videoWedding.flv—Flash Video file, including cue points

SkinUnderAllNoVolNoCaptionNoFull. swf—Contains elements used in the video playback controls

stylesSite.css—Cascading Style Sheet used to format text in the Info section

textInfo.txt—file with HTML-formatted text for the Info section

picsGallery—Directory containing image files for the Gallery section

Once you've copied all these files into the site_files folder, you're ready to upload them using your FTP application and instructions from your Web hosting company or Internet service provider.

When you're done uploading, be sure to view your site via a browser and confirm that everything is working as it should.

That's it! You've successfully created and published a Web site using Flash. Now you have the know-how to create attractive, useful, Flash-based Web sites all on your own. Enjoy!

index

index

index

145

index